BETTER HOMES AND GARDENS®

## Step·By·Step Successful Gardening

# Herb Gardens

Catriona Tudor Erler

Better Homes and Gardens® Books
Des Moines

BETTER HOMES AND GARDENS® BOOKS
An Imprint of Meredith® Books

*Step-By-Step Successful Gardening:*
*Herb Gardens*
Senior Editor: Marsha Jahns
Production Manager: Douglas Johnston

Vice President and Editorial Director: Elizabeth P. Rice
Executive Editor: Kay Sanders
Managing Editor: Christopher Cavanaugh
Art Director: Ernest Shelton

President, Book Group: Joseph J. Ward
Vice President, Retail Marketing: Jamie L. Martin
Vice President, Direct Marketing: Timothy Jarrell

Meredith Corporation
Chairman of the Executive Committee: E. T. Meredith III
Chairman of the Board and Chief Executive Officer:
    Jack D. Rehm
President and Chief Operating Officer: William T. Kerr

*Produced by* ROUNDTABLE PRESS, INC.
Directors: Susan E. Meyer, Marsha Melnick
Executive Editor: Amy T. Jonak
Editorial Director: Anne Halpin
Senior Editor: Jane Mintzer Hoffman
Design: Brian Sisco, Susan Evans, Sisco & Evans, New York
Photo Editor: Marisa Bulzone
Assistant Photo Editor: Carol Sattler
Encyclopedia Editor: Henry W. Art and Storey Communi-
    cations, Inc., Pownal, Vermont
Horticultural Consultant: Christine M. Douglas
Copy Editor: Sue Heinemann
Proofreader: Cathy Peck
Assistant Editor: Alexis Wilson
Step-by-Step Photography: Derek Fell
Garden Plans: Elayne Sears and Storey Communications, Inc.

All of us at Meredith® Books are dedicated to providing you with the information and ideas you need for successful gardening. We guarantee your satisfaction with this book for as long as you own it. If you have any questions, comments, or suggestions, please write to us at:

MEREDITH® BOOKS, *Garden Books*
Editorial Department, RW240
1716 Locust St.
Des Moines, IA 50309-3023

If you would like to order additional copies of any of our books, call 1-800-678-2803 or check with your local bookstore.

Library of Congress Catalog Card Number: 94-74289
ISBN: 0-696-20209-3

The information in this book is intended for reference only and should not be used as a substitute for medical care. Do not attempt to diagnose or treat yourself for any symptoms without the assistance of a health-care professional.

STEP-BY-STEP SUCCESSFUL GARDENING

# Herb Gardens

# The World of Herbs

*O*f all the specialty plants people collect and grow, herbs probably have the largest number of devotees. People grow herbs because they are useful in the home, beautiful in the garden, and rich in legend, tradition, and superstition. • This book presents a clear and interesting summary of the primary facts home gardeners need to know to successfully design with, grow, and use these fascinating plants. You will find ideas and guidelines for creating both formal and informal herb gardens, as well as for incorporating herbs into ornamental beds and vegetable plots. In addition, there is detailed information on planting and caring for herbs, as well as helpful lists of herbs that are suited for specific climatic conditions and uses. • Most herbs are easy to grow and propagate. This book explains how to grow herbs from seeds, cuttings, and layering, as well as how to care for herbs during cold winter months. You'll also discover how to harvest and use your plants. Let this book be your passport into the wonderful world of herbs.

## Mints

*Mint is available in hundreds of varieties, each with different growth patterns and subtly different flavors. Peppermint, from which menthol is distilled, has a familiar sharp taste and has been used as an antiseptic, a digestive aid, and to repel flies and insects. Spearmint has a tangy taste and is a wonderful accompaniment to lamb, veal, carrots, and peas. It makes a refreshing tea and is pretty as a garnish. Snippings are delicious in a green or fruit salad or sprinkled over vanilla ice cream.*

*Other kinds of mint include orange bergamot mint, which has a citrusy flavor; apple or woolly mint, which has an apple fragrance and makes a good ground cover; and Corsican mint, which has a rich peppermint flavor and makes an excellent ground cover resembling baby's-tears.*

The world of herbs includes a diverse range of plants: some annual, others perennial; some edible, others valued for their fragrance or medicinal properties. Herbs come in a vast range of sizes. Tiny Corsican mint plants can root and flourish in the knothole of a tree or between flagstones in a path; dill and fennel grow tall and make good background plants; and sweet bay is a tree that can reach 40 feet high at maturity. The great differences between many of the plants considered herbs may cause you to wonder just what an herb is and how an herb differs from a spice.

The word "herb" comes from the Latin *herba*, which means "grass" or "green crop." This definition could be taken to mean any green-growing plant we harvest. The *Oxford English Dictionary* defines "herb" as "a plant of which the stem does not become woody and persistent (as in a shrub or a tree), but remains more or less soft and succulent, and dies down to the ground (or entirely) after flowering." The dictionary follows with a second definition: "Applied to plants of which the leaves, or stems and leaves, are used for food or medicine, or in some way for their scent or flavor."

Both *OED* definitions are limiting. While most herbs are herbaceous (nonwoody), there are exceptions, such as the bay tree *(Laurus nobilis)*. Also, while the leaves and stems of many herbs are usable, the dictionary definition overlooks the value of flowers, roots, and seeds. Horseradish *(Armoracia rusticana)*, which is prized for the unique flavor of its root, is a valuable culinary herb, and herbs such as dill, anise, and fennel are valued for both their foliage and seeds.

In this book we will define an herb as most herb growers define it—a plant that is useful to people.

In contrast to herbs, the word "spice" comes from the Latin *species*, meaning "ally." Spices complement our foods, and many help preserve them. While the entire plant is recognized as an herb, generally just the part of the plant that is used as flavoring or preservative, such as the seed or bark, is considered the spice.

People have been using herbs throughout history. Archaeologists have unearthed Egyptian papyruses dating back to about 1700 B.C. that record the medicinal use of many herbs, especially garlic. The Greek physician Hippocrates (c. 460–377 B.C.), considered the father of medicine, categorized foods and herbs by their qualities of hot, cold, dry, or damp. Thyme and hyssop were considered warm, dry herbs good for treating phlegm and chest ailments; burdock and figwort, classified as cool and dry, were used to ease gout or diarrhea. Cool, moist plants such as rhubarb, violets, and dandelions were used to treat bad tempers and liver disorders. This information was codified in A.D. 78, when Pedanius Dioscorides, a Greek physician working in Rome, wrote his text *De Materia Medica*, which became the standard medical reference for about 1,500 years.

The Chinese use of herbs also dates back thousands of years, with extant records from as long ago as about 2500 B.C. and legend tracing use of herbs to even earlier. Like the Greeks, the Chinese took a holistic view of the body and saw illness as a sign of disharmony in the whole person. Their doctors strove to restore balance, enabling the body's natural healing mechanisms to work properly.

During the Middle Ages in Europe, the church took over the role of healing. The nuns and monks in monasteries cultivated "physic gardens" planted with herbs believed to have healing properties, and treatments were administered by the religious orders.

*Use freshly harvested herbs, such as the sage, dill, basil, chamomile, parsley, and chives shown here, to add a burst of flavor to your meals.*

### Monastery Gardens

*During the Middle Ages, cloister or courtyard gardens in European monasteries were planted with herbs and plants that had medicinal value. The monks and nuns in religious orders ministered to both body and soul.*

*The most famous examples of monastery gardens in the United States are the three courtyard gardens at the Cloisters, a museum in New York City. Each garden follows a geometric plan with plants that were well known and grown in medieval times. The gardens also feature raised beds, wattle fences, and central ornaments such as fountains or wellheads.*

Their herbal remedies often included religious incantations along with the prescriptions.

With the advent of the printing press in the fifteenth century and increased literacy, radical thinkers such as the physician William Turner began writing herbals in English so that "the apothecaries and old wives that gather herbs" would clearly understand the Latin prescriptions. Turner is considered the father of English botany, and his book, *A New Herball* (1551), is remarkable not only for its information on the medicinal value of herbs, but also for its groundbreaking work in British botanical scholarship. Forty-six years later, in 1597, botanist John Gerard published his *Herball, or Generall Historie of Plantes*, which lists plants found in the British Isles along with their cultivation requirements and uses. Much of what he wrote was based on his own gardening experiences (he grew 1,000 plants in his London garden), although a lot of the plant descriptions were plagiarized from the 1554 herbal of the Dutch botanist Junius Rembert Dodoens.

In 1652 Nicholas Culpeper outraged the College of Physicians by translating their *Pharmacopoeia* into English so that anyone could collect herbal medicines in the wild, rather than paying the inflated apothecaries' fees. As a result of this controversial book, the battle lines were clearly drawn between the physicians and apothecaries and the "herb wives" as to who should have control over prescribing and dispensing medicine. The conflict continued through the seventeenth and eighteenth centuries as the university-trained physicians and apothecaries gradually gained dominance over the herb wives.

While there are those that may scoff at some of the medicinal advice written in these herbals, many of the remedies have been validated by scientific research. As early as 1775, Dr. William Withering began performing experiments with foxglove *(Digitalis* spp.*)* after determining that it was the effective ingredient in an old family recipe for heart failure. He published his findings in 1785, and his work formed the basis for the modern administration of digitalis as treatment for heart disease.

Although most people do not depend solely on herbs for their source of healing drugs, there are as many reasons to grow herbs today as there were in past centuries. Herbs are a marvelous asset in the garden, whether you plan to harvest herbs for the kitchen or medicine cabinet; for cosmetics and soothing bath ingredients; for sachets, potpourris, and other scented novelties; for wreaths and other floral displays; or for natural dyes. Many herbs do double or triple duty in the garden, proving valuable as ornamental plants, as cooking ingredients, and as aids in pest control. Their wonderful scents attract bees and butterflies (as well as people), adding another dimension to the pleasure of the garden.

As a bonus, most herbs are extremely easy to grow. With a few exceptions, they will perform satisfactorily in mediocre to poor soil (although they do better in good conditions), and few pests or diseases bother them. Whether you devote a part of your garden entirely to herbs, mix them with ornamentals in a flower garden, or place them in pots on the kitchen windowsill, you will find that herbs are fascinating and rewarding plants to grow.

The Cloisters in New York City has three courtyard gardens featuring plants popular in medieval times. These gardens are superb examples of monastery gardens.

# CHAPTER 1

# Designing Your Herb Garden

*h*erbs are a diverse group of plants that have ornamental as well as practical properties, and you can find a place for at least one or two herbs in almost any garden. You can mix herbs in with other plants or keep them together in their own garden. • Even in a dedicated herb garden there is room for creativity in your design. You might, for example, feature separate beds for culinary plants, medicinal herbs, dyes, and fragrances. • An herb garden can be as small as a single plant in a pot or as large as a field. It can be an informal, exuberant place bursting with plants, or it can have a formal, structured design. Some herbs produce dramatic flowers; others have fascinating foliage. Enjoy mulling over the wealth of possibilities as you think about the herb garden that best meets your needs.

# Choosing the Best Site

*A surprising number of herbs flourish in shady environments. Lady's-mantle (foreground) and chives (with purple flowers) are especially good choices for shady gardens.*

When choosing the best spot to grow your herbs, consider both the plants' needs and your own. Most herbs are sun lovers that require good drainage, moderately good soil, and neutral to slightly alkaline pH (see sidebars on pages 56 and 57 for lists of herbs for shady locations and wet situations). Since they also tend to be drought tolerant, you can locate them farther from a watering source than other, thirstier plants. *Your* needs may include easy access from the kitchen to the herb garden for culinary plants, creating a beautiful view to see from a window in the house, installing a ground cover on a steep slope, or finding fragrant plants to enhance a sitting area.

In addition to the physical requirements of the herbs you plan to grow, think about your design preferences when you choose the site. If you want a formal herb garden, you need a level site or a hillside terraced into several flat spaces. The traditional knot garden in particular demands a level spot, ideally underneath an upstairs window or balcony, where you can view the garden, with its fascinating pattern, from above. Informal gardens, by nature, are less rigorous about site demands. Beautiful cottage-style herb gardens can be planted across the face of a hillside or on other uneven ground.

It's not essential to devote one site entirely to herbs. Many herbs produce lovely flowers and are well worth adding to an ornamental border. Edible herbs

Most of the well-known kitchen herbs, such as parsley, basil, sage, and rosemary, thrive in sunny gardens.

are welcome additions to your vegetable garden. Some of the shrubby herbs, such as santolina, can be pruned and will adapt well as low-growing hedges. And the shorter plants make excellent edging material for a bed, while creeping thyme and other low growers make superb ground covers.

To determine the best site in your garden for herbs, notice how many hours of sunlight a day the spot you have in mind gets. Six to seven hours of light a day is considered a minimum for plants that require full sun.

Ideally the garden spot should be protected from wind. Consider planting a hedge or building a fence to enclose the garden on at least the north and east sides. The hedge can be the classic dark green of yew, box, or leyland cypress, but is not limited to those possibilities. Rugosa roses, for example, are excellent as billowing hedges, especially for herb gardens.

If you are concerned about the soil draining properly, dig a hole the projected size of the plant's root system, fill it with water, allow it to drain, and fill it a second time. The water level in the hole should have dropped at least ¼ inch during the first hour for adequate drainage. If it doesn't, you should add organic material to amend the soil and improve the drainage, install drain tiles, or create raised beds in which to garden. For most herbs, the beds need to be raised only 8 to 12 inches high.

# Formal Gardens

*T*he tradition of formal gardens dates back to the earliest recorded garden design in ancient Egypt. During the Middle Ages, herb gardens were often divided into distinct beds, either squares or strips, with a different herb planted in each area so that the person harvesting wouldn't confuse the plants and perhaps administer the wrong herbal medicine to the patient.

The early American settlers brought with them the traditional garden designs they knew in Europe. Life was hard, and gardens were planted for practical rather than aesthetic purposes. The settlers grew plants that were useful as food, medicine, or dyes. Even during the later colonial years in America, when life was slightly less harsh, gardens were functional creations (except for the very wealthy). The herb garden generally was placed near the kitchen for quick access, and annual herbs and vegetables were planted together. Raised rectangular planting areas were the popular arrangement for garden beds. The beds were usually laid out in quadrants intersected by paths. These beds were often bordered with box or winter savory. A tight picket fence, along with small fruit trees and berry bushes, defined the perimeter of the garden. As in medieval European gardens, medicinal herbs were planted together in distinct rows to avoid confusion. The raised beds, which originated in Roman times, made it slightly easier to work in the garden because the gardener didn't have to bend over so far, and the beds also solved any problems of inadequate soil or drainage in the garden.

*Generally, colonial-style herb gardens feature raised beds arranged in symmetrical geometric patterns.*

Colonial Williamsburg in Virginia is an excellent place to see a variety of colonial-style gardens. Note that each bed has a border with a mass-planting of a low-growing herb.

# *Formal Gardens* CONTINUED

**TROUBLESHOOTING
TIP**

*If you are re-creating a
period garden for a historic
house, do your research to
avoid common mistakes.
For example, split-rail fences
were used in the past to
enclose fields but not
gardens. A picket fence is
historically accurate. Herbs
were mixed with flowers and
vegetables, rarely planted
alone as an herb garden.*

Throughout the centuries, the details of formal garden design have varied according to the needs and
aesthetic taste of the era. However, there is always an
underlying regard for the geometric principles of scale
and proportion. During the Renaissance architects
worked out highly specific guidelines for correct proportion and geometry in their building designs, and
these principles were applied to garden layout. We
can see the results of these codified formulas in the
carefully balanced relationships in designs from the
sixteenth, seventeenth, and even eighteenth centuries.
Although today these rules are no longer strictly followed, the underlying principles of geometry and proportion still guide the design of formal herb gardens.
A related component of formal design is the use of
symmetry.

As a general rule, a formal garden is laid out in
straight lines with the design symmetrically repeated
on both sides. A central path down the middle of the
garden serves as an axis dividing the garden into two
matched sections. If you wish to include some shrubs
or trees as accents in a formal herb garden, plant
them in pairs or sets of four, perhaps marking the
four corners of the garden or flanking the path at
both ends.

In addition to enhancing the sense of symmetry,
paired accent shrubs also provide pattern, another
characteristic of well-designed formal gardens. Pruned
into geometric shapes such as pyramids, globes, rec-
tangles, or spirals, the shrubs add visual interest as
well as a subliminal reference to the geometric principles that govern the garden's layout. Andrew Wilson,
chairman of the Society of Garden Designers in
England, defines pattern in the garden as "a visual
system which relies on the repetition and combination
of shapes." Although he cautions against too much

**1** *To create a raised herb garden bed, measure
the space carefully, and mark the outside borders
with posts and string.*

**5** *Level the soil with a rake, breaking up any
large clods. Water thoroughly to allow the soil to
settle and to prepare it for plants.*

**2** Dig out the existing weeds and grass, removing several inches of soil. Cut a clean, straight edge along the border of the bed.

**3** Build the raised box for the bed using cedar posts (as shown here), landscape ties, boards, bricks, cement blocks, or any suitable material.

**4** Fill the new bed with good-quality topsoil. Don't waste time and money on poor-quality, heavy soil that will drain slowly.

**6** Transplant potted herbs into the bed, or sow seeds. In this garden, different varieties of basil seedlings will make a colorful display.

**7** Plant seedlings, tamping down the soil around the roots. Be sure to space the plants with enough room to allow for their growth.

**8** Water thoroughly. Once the plants are established, they will need less water. Seeds should be kept moist until they sprout.

# *Formal Gardens* CONTINUED

repetition, which can become monotonous, he warns that a lack of repetition makes it impossible to discern any pattern, or sense of order. According to Wilson, symmetrical groups of plants give a formal garden design a sense of balance and equilibrium.

The overall division of space in a formal garden creates the initial pattern, which can be emphasized by giving the beds distinct edges. You can also set up patterns with the paths' paving material, as well as the plants you use in the garden. A formal garden with a clearly visible pattern is particularly exciting to see from above. If possible, situate your formal herb garden where it can be seen from upstairs windows, a high balcony or deck, or an upper terraced level.

A vista is another dynamic element in formal garden design. It can link different sections of a larger garden, as well as entice a visitor to move toward the

accented view. Ideally, a formal herb garden should have a connected relationship to other parts of the garden and house. The central path running through the garden might be an axis continuing from a window in the house or leading into another part of the garden. If the formal herb garden is a private place with hedges or walls to contain the scents, then a bench, arbor, or garden gate makes a wonderful focal point at the end of the axis, creating a satisfying, albeit short, vista.

The geometric basis of formal garden design may seem constraining, but there is wide scope for creativity. You might, for example, compose a garden of four square beds intersected by paths, design a large rectangular bed bordered with a path and half-circle beds at each end, create a series of triangular beds, establish a paved or planted circular space in the

*Formal, geometric gardens do not have to look old-fashioned. Although classic in its formality, this garden has a sleek, modern look that is enhanced by the simple lines of the bench.*

*This garden has many of the elements of an old formal garden: the symmetrical geometric design, the pathways, and a tree in the center of each bed to break the dominant horizontal lines.*

### Edging Materials

*Edging defines the garden boundary and acts as a frame, setting off whatever is planted inside. If the garden path is paved with loose material, the edging also keeps the path in its place. A low hedge around the bed keeps plants inside their bounds.*

*You can edge an herb garden with wood, stone, large shells, or bricks. A very elegant—and expensive— edging can be made from reproductions of Victorian terra-cotta or glazed and fired clay figurines. These come in different designs, often scalloped.*

*You can also use the herbs themselves for edging. Consider low-growing plants such as chives, thyme, parsley, dwarf hyssop, winter savory, or alpine strawberries. Southernwood, lavender, and rosemary also work well if pruned to stay low and bushy.*

# *Formal Gardens* CONTINUED

center with four beds extending to the corners of the garden, or try hundreds of other combinations and variations of geometric patterns. You can even design a round garden, dividing it into sections with radiating paths that converge in the center. The result looks like a wagon wheel, with the paths providing easy access to all parts of the garden. Or modify this design into a small "pizza garden," with herbs used to flavor pizza, such as basil, oregano, and marjoram, planted in each wedge.

The best way to come up with a design that you like is to measure the dimensions of the space you plan to plant, and draw it on graph paper. Then try sketching different designs on tracing-paper overlays until you arrive at the one that pleases you most. It is also helpful to look at photographs of formal gardens to see what has worked for other people. You might combine two designs from books or magazines into an original one of your own. Just as artists and writers are influenced by famous works from the past, many well-known and successful gardeners find inspiration in gardens created by others.

*True to formal design, this circular herb garden is centered within the rectangular garden "room," as well as on the path leading from the adjoining garden.*

**1** *Choose a large, spoked wheel to create a cartwheel herb garden.*

**2** *Position the wheel in an appropriate spot in your garden. Choose a site with good soil.*

**3** *Select plants that look good together or whose flavorings have a common theme.*

**4** *Plant herbs between each spoke, allowing enough space for each to grow to maturity.*

**5** *The growing plants should fill in the ground without obscuring the decorative wheel.*

# *Formal Gardens* CONTINUED

**Plants for Edging Knot Gardens**

*Herbs lend themselves well to the intricate, twisted designs of formal knot gardens. For a knot garden, select plants that are evergreen and can be planted close enough together to form an unbroken line. The plants should also take pruning well. Good choices include boxwood (Buxus sempervirens, both green and golden varieties), germander (Teucrium chamaedrys), lavender (Lavandula), lavender cotton (Santolina chamaecyparissus), rosemary (Rosmarinus), and thyme (Thymus vulgaris).*

As a finishing touch, place an ornament or other garden accent in the center of the formal herb garden to add interest and to emphasize the geometry of your design. Traditional possibilities include bee skeps that look like inverted woven baskets, armillary spheres, sundials, birdbaths, wells, urns, statues, and fountains. If none of those ideas appeals—or if they are too expensive—plant a yew or boxwood in the center of the garden and prune it as a topiary in either a geometric or a fanciful shape. Another idea is to grow a bay tree in a beautiful pot placed right in the center of the garden. Cold-climate gardeners can bring the potted tree indoors during winter.

Within a formal structure it's possible to have informal plantings. Many well-known English gardens are designed with a strong framework of walls, hedges, paths, beds, and borders (the bones of the garden), but are then planted in a loose, romantic, cottage-garden style. The English novelist and garden writer Vita Sackville-West described her garden at Sissinghurst Castle in Kent as "the strictest formality of design combined with a strict informality in planting." The French artist Claude Monet's popular garden in Giverny is another example where the very linear design of the beds is softened by profuse plantings

*This classic knot garden growing at Agecroft Hall, a fifteenth-century country manor in Richmond, Virginia, features plants of different colors and textures arranged to resemble intertwining ribbons.*

Gravel used for garden paths or in knot gardens comes in many different colors, sizes, and textures. Choose a gravel that best complements the size and style of your garden.

**1** For a knot garden, use sand or lime on level soil to outline your design. Geometric precision is essential. Use string and pegs to achieve straight lines.

**2** Before planting, position all your plants along the lines, making sure the spacing is correct and the right plants are on the correct loops of the knot.

**3** Center each plant on the guideline, and space them evenly apart. If a root ball is tight, break it apart to encourage healthy, spreading growth.

**4** Spread colored gravel within the spaces of your knot to help keep down weeds and to enhance the design. Use different colors to delineate separate loops.

# *Formal Gardens* CONTINUED

**Colored Mulches**

*A wide variety of materials can be used as colored mulches in a knot garden. Possibilities include* **yellow:** *clay, sand;* **gray:** *gravel, pebbles;* **red:** *crushed bricks, broken pots;* **brown:** *bark;* **black:** *lava rock, charcoal;* **white:** *gravel, crushed oyster shells, marble chips;* **sparkle:** *bits of ground glass.*

*For an attractive look, stick to natural materials in earth tones, and plan to renew the mulch annually to keep it in perfect condition.*

that spill out onto the paths. In fact, this combination of formal design with informal plantings is particularly suited to herbs, which often grow with more exuberance than control.

Knot gardens are a special type of formal herb garden that became popular in the sixteenth century. Believed to be originally inspired by the patterns in Persian carpets, knot gardens are made up of different colored plants that grow as low hedges and that are planted to look like ribbons running over and under each other in an elaborate design or knot. The spaces are either mass-planted with low-growing annuals or filled in with different colored stones, shells, and marble chips. Plants typically used to create knot gardens include germander, rosemary, thyme, dwarf lavender, lavender cotton *(Santolina chamaecyparissus)*, and boxwood. Although these plants are all aromatic or fragrant, you would not harvest them from the knot garden. Unlike most herb gardens, knot gardens are used strictly for ornamental purposes—except, perhaps, for the prunings.

*In this formal garden, the geometric, symmetrical beds give a strong sense of order and design, while plants spilling over the edges soften the look and add charm.*

It is a geometric challenge to create a knot garden. The first step is to draw your design on paper. For inspiration, turn to books on formal garden design or other garden books that include photographs of knot gardens. For ancient sources, look for books in antiquarian bookstores or libraries that have a selection of old garden books. One good source of garden designs popular in the sixteenth century is *The Gardener's Labyrinth* by Thomas Hill. For more contemporary inspiration, try reading *Classic Garden Design*, by the English garden writer Rosemary Verey, or *Creating Formal Gardens*, by Roy Strong.

Perhaps the best way to find ideas for a knot garden is to see one for yourself. In the United States, there are several knot gardens that you can visit in gardens open to the public, such as the New York Botanical Garden in New York City; Filoli, near San Francisco; the herb garden at the U.S. National Arboretum in Washington, D.C.; Well-Sweep Herb Farm in Port Murray, New Jersey; the Chicago Botanical Garden, in Glencoe, Illinois; and Agecroft Hall in Richmond, Virginia.

Although the design possibilities are limitless, bear in mind that you are more likely to succeed if the design for your knot garden is not too complicated. As a rule of thumb, if the inside of the pattern is intricate, the edges should be simple, and vice versa.

Once you have your final design on paper, you must transfer it to the garden. Geometric accuracy is essential for the finished product to look right, and the site should be level. The tools you need to achieve straight lines, pure arcs, and true circles include lime or sand to mark the lines, string, a tape measure, and pegs. Fill a bottle with the lime or sand, and use it to evenly mark the lines. If you need to make circles or curves, tie string to a peg at one end and the bottle at the other, then let the bottle be the "pencil" for your compass.

Once the lines are defined, plant along them, spacing the plants close enough together so that when they are nearly mature they will form an unbroken hedge. Where the lines intersect, decide which plants are meant to appear to be going over and which under. You can enhance the woven look by shearing the plants closer to the ground on the line that's meant to be going under. Also emphasize the different threads of the knot with different colored plants—interplanting, for example, gray lavender, golden box (such as *Buxus sempervirens* 'Aureovariegata'), green box, and blue-gray santolina. Fill the blank spaces between the lines of plants with colored gravel, crushed bricks or clay pots, oyster shells, or charcoal, depending on the colors you prefer. To avoid a jarring appearance, however, it is best to stick with materials that have natural earth tones.

The same principles used to lay out a knot garden apply to any formal garden. To be successful, the design must be symmetrical, and the lines must be true. Remember that the layout and proportions are based on the classic designs of the Renaissance. But do not be intimidated by this. With accurate measuring and careful planting, you can create a formal herb garden that has an appealing sense of structure and balance.

**E A R T H • W I S E TIP**

*To keep down weeds in a knot garden, place a ¼-inch-thick layer of newspaper underneath colored mulch. Don't use black plastic underneath mulch because it will suffocate the soil. The newspaper, which is organic, will break down and ultimately improve the soil.*

# *Informal Styles*

**TIMESAVING TIP**

*If you are creating an irregularly shaped garden bed from scratch, use a garden hose to outline the configuration you have in mind. By using a hose, rather than immediately starting to dig, you can play with the different design possibilities, changing the shape at will. This is a good way to see instantly how your future garden will look.*

An informal herb garden or an informal garden that is an eclectic mix of plants that includes herbs is ideal for the person who doesn't have a suitably level, sunny space for a formal herb garden. It's also great for those whose interest in different plants is bigger than their garden, making them reluctant to devote a large space solely to herbs. And it will appeal to those who want a freer ambience than the controlled, regulated look of a formal garden. Here, curved lines and asymmetric plantings dominate, in contrast to the straight, geometric lines and symmetry of formal designs.

Although a good informal garden design looks natural, paradoxically it is much harder to create than a formal look. There are fewer hard-and-fast rules to rely on in creating an informal garden, and few traditions that have stood the test of time. However, certain design principles, such as repeated planting patterns and effective texture combinations, do apply to informal gardens. The goal is to create a sense of balance and continuity between the plants and different spaces in the garden.

There are many ways to use herbs in an informal garden. Instead of devoting matching rectangular beds to herbs in a formal style, you can fill a free-form bed full of different herbs. Or plant the same irregularly shaped bed with a mixture of flowers, herbs, shrubs, trees, and vegetables. You can include flowering herbs in a flower garden or culinary herbs in a vegetable garden. By extending your palette of plants to the huge world of ornamentals and other edibles, you give yourself a wonderful array of choices for color (both in leaf and flower), texture, plant form, and habit. In a well-designed informal garden, these qualities, rather than geometry and symmetry, are the dominating features.

An informal herb garden might be as small as a pot planted with basil or parsley by the kitchen door, or it might be slightly larger, with all the space near the door crammed full of useful plants: herbs, flowers for cutting, and vegetables.

Cottage gardens, typically planted around small, unpretentious homes, are a wonderful informal environment for herbs. In these gardens, a wide variety of plants, both edible and ornamental, are jammed together in a mixture of colors, shapes, and sizes. Traditional spacing recommendations are ignored, and the plants are given just enough space to grow to maturity. Low-growing plants are tucked under the skirts of taller specimens, and spring plants that die down as hot weather approaches are overplanted with summer bloomers. In this closely planted environment, weeds cannot easily gain a foothold. The secret to the success of such a high-density style of gardening is good, fertile soil that allows all the plants to grow vigorously in happy profusion.

Although informal in planting style, cottage gardens are tied to tradition. They are usually enclosed with a picket fence, stone wall, or hedge. The beds are generally divided by a path leading from the garden gate to the front door of the house. But you can adapt the general cottage garden look to just about any situation. Plant an island bed full of herbs, flowers, fruits, and shrubs to look like a cottage garden. Or try dense, cottage-style plantings on hillsides, where it is awkward to weed. A cottage garden is also the perfect approach for plant enthusiasts who don't have very much room to garden. Given the proper environment and care, a remarkable number of plants can be sustained in a small space.

*Caraway, a biennial, is ideal for a meadow garden of herbs because it self-seeds, readily establishing itself in a field. However, it does not transplant well.*

*Plant herbs near a doorway, where you can easily reach them for harvesting. You will also enjoy their scent every time you walk by the door.*

# Herbs and Flowers

*Herbs are a wonderful addition to flower gardens. Many produce dramatic flowers of their own, and others have attractive foliage. This garden includes tarragon, lavender, and catmint.*

Although many herbs bear tiny, insignificant flowers, others produce bold blossoms that compare favorably with those of ornamental plants. Many of these herbs, which are also useful in cooking or medicine, deserve consideration for places of honor in your flower beds.

A prime candidate for a sunny flower bed or herbaceous border is sage. Sage has a long history of medicinal and culinary importance, and it is also an excellent, hardy garden perennial. The most common sage, *Salvia officinalis*, produces tall spikes of lavender flowers in late spring. The cultivar 'Albiflora' has white blossoms.

Another excellent choice for a flower garden is anise hyssop *(Agastache foeniculum)*. An upright plant, it produces showy, anise-scented, lilac-blue flowers in late summer.

Legend claims that the Greek hero Achilles used yarrow to stop bleeding and heal wounds during the Trojan War, thus explaining the plant's genus name, *Achillea*. Although once considered a plant with extraordinary healing powers, today yarrow is appreciated more for its ornamental properties. It has beautifully textured dark green or gray-green foliage and large, bold flower clusters in golden yellow, pink, or white. Depending on the species, plants will grow anywhere from 6 inches to 5 feet tall. Fern-leaf yarrow *(Achillea filipendulina)* is perhaps the most popular for fresh and dried flowers. It produces spectacular yellow flower heads up to 5 to 6 inches wide.

*The attractive gray foliage of lavender cotton* (Santolina) *is enhanced by little yellow buttonlike flowers that bloom from late spring to early summer.*

*Lavender hedges flanking the path add an attractive and delightfully scented element to this garden.*

To brighten your garden and perfume the air, try English lavender *(Lavandula angustifolia)*. Loved for its scent, lavender was used in ancient times to perfume baths and burned as incense to fumigate hospitals. Its Latin name stems from *lavare*, which means "to wash." Lavender plants grow in dense clumps, creating floral pools of purple in a border. Or plant them close together in a row to form a dwarf hedge. The silvery grayish green foliage makes a handsome display, and during the late spring to early summer bloom season, the flower spikes dominate the planting in various shades of purple, or even white, depending on the hybrid.

The smallest members of the onion family, chives *(Allium schoenoprasum)* are valuable both for their culinary and ornamental properties. Both the tubular leaves and lavender-pink flower balls are edible. Growing in clumps up to 18 inches tall, they are excellent planted as a border to flower or herb beds. Chives bloom in late spring to midsummer on stalks that stand above the leafy clumps. Their close relatives, garlic chives *(Allium tuberosum)*, bear round clusters of fragrant white flowers in late summer.

# Herbs Underfoot

Several low-growing, spreading herbs tolerate foot traffic and can even withstand being sat upon. The joy of an herbal ground cover is the delicious scent that is released when you step on it. In fact, chamomile seems to flourish under the stress of being walked upon. When chamomile leaves are crushed, they give off an applelike scent.

Consider planting thyme or chamomile as a ground cover between stepping stones or even as the path itself. Vita Sackville-West planted a thyme lawn for her garden at Sissinghurst with white, purple, and pink varieties of *Thymus serpyllum*. It remains green throughout the year, and every July becomes a scented mass of color. She also planted chamomile *(Chamaemelum nobilis)* on a stone seat so that people stopping to sit would be refreshed by the herb's fragrance as they rested. In lieu of a stone garden chair,

you can plant thyme or chamomile in a raised bed at a height that would make a comfortable scented seat. Both herbs also make an excellent low-maintenance carpet on a steep hillside. Mix varieties of creeping thyme with different leaf and flower colors to create a tapestry-like effect.

There are more than 400 types of thyme, many of which are suitable for ground covers. Among the low-growing varieties are *Thymus* 'Annie Hall', with sweet-smelling pink blossoms; *T. pseudolanuginosus*, or woolly thyme, whose green leaves are brushed with a gray-white fuzz; *T. × citriodorus*, which has a lemon scent and is reputed to repel mosquitoes; creeping thyme or mother-of-thyme *(T. praecox* subsp. *arcticus)*, which produces lavender-blue flowers; and a white cultivar, *T. praecox* 'Albus'.

*Creeping thyme makes a fabulous year-round ground cover. Here it is mixed with bugleweed* (Ajuga) *and pinks* (Dianthus) *for a charming medley of low-growing plants.*

**1** When planting between paving stones, first set the stones, then place low-growing herbs between them.

**2** Plant small, young plants between the stones, allowing enough room for them to grow and spread.

**3** In addition to being a decorative element between the paving stones, this apple mint can be harvested.

*Space paving stones so that they are a comfortable distance apart for walking. In between these flagstones are several varieties of creeping thyme. The different variegations of the leaves create a medley of soft green hues. The scents of the herbs are released when the plants are stepped upon.*

# Herbs in Containers

### Herbs for Containers

*The following herbs adapt well to containers: basil, bay (can be trained as a standard topiary), borage, catmint, catnip, chervil, chives, Greek oregano, hyssop, lavender, lemon balm, marjoram, mint, mint marigold, parsley, rosemary (can be trained as a standard), sage, savory, scented geraniums (can be trained as a standard), sorrel, tarragon, and thyme.*

$M$any herbs grow well in containers, both indoors and out, making it possible for people without gardening space to grow herbs and to extend the growing season for tender herbs in cold climates.

There are many reasons for containing herbs. Mint is such an invasive plant that you are wise to grow it in a pot even if you have the garden space for it. You can even grow mint, or other invasive herbs, in containers, and bury the pots in the ground. Gardeners with shade may be able to find one or two sunny spots in the garden for a barrel planted with basil, chives, and oregano. A wooden tub next to the kitchen door planted with herbs may be more convenient to the cook than a hike across the property to the herb garden, or make the herbs even more accessible by growing them inside on a bright kitchen windowsill. Use containers of herbs on the patio to soften the expanse of paving and to scent the sitting area, or put them in a window box so that you can enjoy a pinch of scent every time you open the window.

The possibilities for containers are limited only by your imagination and the growth requirements of the herbs. Plant each pocket of a strawberry jar with a cascading small herb such as creeping thyme, and then top it with an ornamental flowering herb such as feverfew *(Tanacetum parthenium)* or scented geranium. Choose wide, shallow pots for creeping herbs such as oregano, marjoram, thyme, and mint, and herbs with shallow root systems such as chives. Plants with taproots or bulbous roots, such as parsley and onions, require a 6- to 8-inch-deep pot. Shrubby herbs such as rosemary, sage, winter savory, and scented geraniums do well in tubs, although you can grow just one of these plants in a smaller pot.

*Lemongrass, which adapts quite well to a container, should be taken indoors in climates with winter freezes.*

**1** To improve drainage in a strawberry barrel, put a drainage pipe into the center, or use cans punched with holes and both ends removed.

**2** Set the pipe so that its top is level with the can's rim. Fill the barrel with good potting soil. Keep the inside of the center cylinder empty.

**3** For a planter this size, use young plants growing in small, 2- to 3-inch pots to begin planting around the rim of the barrel.

**4** Continue to add plants, such as the sage and basil shown here, placing them close together so that they will grow into a full mass.

**5** Push aside soil from the side holes to make room for the roots of additional plants. Trailing herbs are good choices for side pockets.

**6** Since this is a very dense growing situation, add a mild liquid fertilizer to the water when you water the plants.

# Designing with Plant Heights

**Tall Herbs**

*These plants work best when grown toward the back of the garden or planted as background: angelica, shown above (to 8 feet), bay (40-foot tree, kept much shorter with pruning), beebalm (to 3 feet), dill (to 3 feet), fennel (3 to 4 feet), lemongrass (3 to 4 feet), lovage (4 to 6 feet), mugwort (4 to 6 feet), mullein (to 6 feet), sage (1 to 3 feet, depending on variety), southernwood (3 to 5 feet), sweet cicely (to 3 feet), tansy (to 4 feet), and yarrow (to 3½ feet, some varieties to 5 feet).*

A general rule of thumb in planning flower or herb beds is to put the tallest plants in back, medium-sized plants in the middle of the garden, and shorter ones in front. Low-growing herbs that form masses or clumps, such as lavender, parsley, chives, and santolina, are excellent planted as edgings to outline a garden bed. When you are designing an island garden or a wide bed that can be viewed from both sides, place the tall plants in the center with plant heights gradually diminishing as you move outward toward the perimeter of the bed. Put the lowest plants around the outer edges of a freestanding bed.

Designing gardens of herbs (or gardens of any other plants) with height in mind offers a couple of benefits. First, all the plants in the garden are readily visible to viewers. Second, if the bed is oriented to face south, with taller plants to the north of lower growers, the tall plants won't block the sun and cast shade across the shorter ones.

Of course, every garden design rule is meant to be broken, and you should, above all, design your herb garden to please yourself. Even the experts break the rules. The well-known English gardener and writer Penelope Hobhouse likes to bring some tall plants forward in her gardens, so that they cast a shadow behind them. She prefers plants arranged in a series of heights and valleys to a garden that's very carefully graded.

Another possibility is to have one or more high points in the bed—for example, a stand of tall dill, with lower growing plants clustered around. Garden writer and designer Rosemary Verey's much-photographed laburnum walk at Barnsley House, her home in the Cotswolds in England, is yet another approach to mixing tall and short plants. Along the avenue of laburnum she has planted *Allium*

*aflatunense,* which sends up 3-foot-tall flower stalks, each topped by a cluster of lavender flowers that form a large, lacy globe. These flower heads seem to hover above the hostas and golden lemon balm, which grow as an underplanting. In June, when the laburnum and alliums are in bloom, this shady, plant-lined path is breathtaking.

However you choose to place the tall plants in your herb garden, whether in the front of the beds or in the rear, remember that they give a sense of architectural structure to the design. They also add drama, breaking through the horizontal plane to reach for the sky. Picture a bed of herbs mostly 1 to 3 feet tall punctuated by a clump of fern-leaf yarrow *(Achillea filipendulina)* towering 5 feet high with its fernlike foliage and bright yellow flowers. Licorice-flavored fennel *(Foeniculum vulgare),* with its threadlike leaves and airy flower clusters, is another herb that grows tall. A bronze-leaved form with yellow, pink, and purple flowers is particularly attractive and is seen in more and more flower gardens. Fennel is an excellent choice if you want to experiment with a tall plant toward the front of the bed, because its filigreed foliage gives a filtered view of the plants behind.

While one or two dramatically tall plants shooting up above the rest may work in a design, generally you should group shorter plants in clusters to create pools of leaf color and texture. In a densely planted bed, these low masses will merge with each other and with clumps of taller plants into a harmonic blend of heights, forms, colors, and textures.

When you are planning a bed of herbs of varying heights, work to achieve a pleasing scale and balanced proportions for the garden. If the bed is small, it may be overpowered by a 5-foot-tall yarrow, although a large bed can look fussy if all the plants are small.

*Low-growing purple-leaved sage and marjoram make a colorful border in front of the tall clary sage and white-blooming garlic chives in this garden.*

**Small Herbs**
*Feature these compact plants in the front of the garden, use them for edgings, or grow them in pots or window boxes. You can also use the following herbs to create a pocket garden in an unused corner: miniature basil, boxwood, catnip, chamomile, chives, germander, hyssop, juniper, lavender, lavender cotton, parsley, rosemary, sage, southernwood, sweet woodruff, thyme, violets, winter savory, and wormwood.*

*Low-growing wintergreen (Gaultheria procumbens), shown above, is an excellent ground cover for acid soils. The white summer flowers develop into edible red berries in the fall.*

Your garden will also look unplanned and scattered if plants of too many different heights are randomly situated throughout the bed. As a guide to scale, remember that a bed is well proportioned if it is twice as wide as its tallest plants are high.

Almost any bed, whether formal or informal, benefits from a border of plants along the edge. The border works like a frame, setting off the picture to its best advantage as well as defining the perimeter. Many herbs are excellent as border plants and are often used to edge flower gardens as well as herb gardens. Some good choices for edging are the classic boxwood *(Buxus sempervirens)*, germander *(Teucrium chamaedrys)*, catnip *(Nepeta cataria)*, some varieties of rosemary *(Rosmarinus spp.)*, wormwood *(Artemisia absinthium)*, lamb's-ears *(Stachys byzantina)*, feverfew *(Tanacetum parthenium)*, grass or cottage pinks *(Dianthus plumarius)*, and curly parsley *(Petroselinum crispum)*, as well as creeping plants such as thyme, chamomile, and sweet woodruff *(Galium odoratum)*. Boxwood, catnip, and rosemary need to be pruned to maintain a neat, tailored look.

# Growth Habits

When gardeners talk about growth habits, they are referring to a plant's inclination to grow to a certain height and width. Within those parameters lie other aspects of growth habit. The plant may have a tidy, compact form, or it may sprawl in an open, unkempt manner. The plant may tend to mound or send out shoots that droop at the ends, giving the appearance of fountain sprays. It may send up a tall central stem like a spire or rocket, or be spreading and tall.

You can use the different growth habits of plants to great effect in the garden. Low-growing creepers such as some of the thymes, sweet woodruff, and Roman chamomile are excellent ground covers. Creeping thyme and chamomile can even withstand mild foot traffic, releasing a delicious scent when they are crushed.

Upright, vertical herbs such as fennel *(Foeniculum vulgare)*, anise *(Pimpinella anisum)*, tansy *(Tanacetum vulgare)*, clary sage *(Salvia sclarea)*, mullein *(Verbascum)*, foxgloves *(Digitalis purpurea)*, and some of the taller yarrow *(Achillea)* varieties make excellent background plants in a border and can even act as a screen to block an unsightly view. You might also want to use one as a specimen plant or put it in the center of a bed with shorter plants surrounding it.

Low-growing plants with a mounding habit are excellent for borders and can even be pruned to further emphasize this natural form. Lavender cotton *(Santolina chamaecyparissus)*, English lavender *(Lavandula angustifolia)*, wormwood *(Artemisia absinthium)*, some varieties of rosemary *(Rosmarinus spp.)*, and germander *(Teucrium chamaedrys)* are delightful mounding plants. Also consider catmint *(Nepeta × faassenii)*, which produces lovely blue or lavender flowers. Alternatively, you might consider

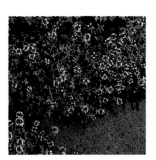

*This thyme spreads readily between paving stones.*

*The spreading varieties of rosemary are ideal for tumbling over walls or dangling out of hanging baskets.*

*Rue is a bushy upright plant with feathery foliage and attractive yellow flowers.*

massing one type of mounding plant to create a ground cover suggesting gently billowing waves.

Old types of shrub roses such as the rugosas *(Rosa rugosa)* have bushy habits, and many of these lovely roses also take on a fountainlike form. These bushy plants are great either in a large mixed bed or planted on their own as specimens. To create an informal hedge, plant them in a row.

Some herbs have untidy growth habits, while others are contained and self-disciplined. Oregano grows in an unruly mass; it is very tasty but not orderly. In contrast, comfrey *(Symphytum officinale)* grows in large, tidy clumps, especially if you cut it back severely each winter and remove root offshoots. Other herbs, such as mint, can become leggy if left to grow rampant, but will form attractive, dense clusters if they are occasionally snipped. As is often the case, regular harvesting improves the appearance of these plants.

When designing an herb garden, take advantage of the wide variety of forms and growth habits to create an appealing scene. Put tall, upright plants toward the back of a border. Tuck unruly plants among those with more tidy habits, which can help hold them up and possibly even contain them. Mix and match the different forms so that each enhances the other and perhaps compensates for its flaws.

### Thymes

*Ranging in form from low-to-the-ground creepers that make superb ground covers to upright varieties that grow in foot-high clumps, there are more than 400 catalogued species of thyme. In addition to the flavor and scent of common thyme* (Thymus vulgaris), *which we are familiar with from the spice jar, thyme varieties come with fragrances resembling camphor, lemon, caraway, coconut, and nutmeg. Some have bright green leaves; others have gray, purple, variegated yellow-and-green, or even furry leaves. Many produce masses of attractive flowers that attract bees in droves.*

*If you want to use thyme as a ground cover, try planting creeping thyme* (T. praecox), *which has pink flowers; coconut thyme* (T. pulegioides 'Coccineus'), *which has pink flowers and dark green leaves; or woolly thyme* (T. pseudolanuginosus), *which has silvery gray leaves and a woolly texture.*

*Clary sage is a tall, upright biennial growing as high as 5 feet. It will self-sow if the flowers, which grow the second year, are allowed to go to seed.*

*When in bloom in early summer, Spanish lavender* (Lavandula stoechas) *resembles a bursting firework. The plants grow 1 to 2 feet high.*

# Leaf Colors and Textures

### Herbs with Variegated Leaves

*Variegated herbs have leaf patterns in more than one color. Some are listed below.*

*Mint: orange mint (Mentha × piperita var. citrata) has dark green leaves edged with purple; pineapple mint (M. suaveolens 'Variegata') has green leaves with white patches.*

*Sage: golden sage (Salvia officinalis 'Aurea') has green leaves edged with yellow; purple sage (S. officinalis 'Purpurea') has green leaves edged in purplish red; tricolor sage (S. officinalis 'Tricolor') has cream, purplish red, and pink leaves.*

*Thyme: lemon thyme (Thymus × citriodorus 'Aureus') has green and yellow leaves; silver lemon thyme (T. citriodorus 'Argenteus') has leaves variegated with green and silver; silver thyme (T. vulgaris 'Argenteus') has silver and green leaves; golden thyme (T. vulgaris 'Aureus') has yellow and green leaves.*

Leaves come in many colors and textures that can be effective design tools in the garden. Use gray and silver foliage to make bright red flowers look even more dramatic, or soften pastel pink and blue blooms with a gray border. In a seaside or southwestern garden, gray foliage can also help cut the constant glare of the bright sun. Try putting purple basil, with its dark purple foliage veined with pinkish red, next to borage, with its clear blue-violet flowers. Choose the bright red flowers of beebalm *(Monarda didyma)* to pick out the hint of magenta in the green, cream, and pink leaves of tricolor sage.

Multicolored leaves, such as those of tricolor sage, are known as variegated (see the sidebar on this page). Common color combinations of variegated herbs include green with golden yellow, cream, white, pink, or silver. A plant with variegated leaves can be a striking accent and conversation piece in the garden, but be careful not to overdo it.

Even among solid-colored leaves, the shades of color are remarkable. Some plants have gray or silver foliage; others, such as purple basil and perilla *(P. frutescens)*, bear dark red or purple leaves. The new leaves of bronze fennel are a rusty red, the same color that runs through the veins in the stems. Lemon thyme has yellow-green leaves, and golden sage glows with yellow.

*The frilly leaves of Purple Ruffles basil are a striking color and texture contrast to a white-flowering sage cultivar.*

*This peppermint geranium (Pelargonium tomentosum) has lobed leaves that are green on the edges with deep purple centers.*

*Tricolor sage has a lovely leaf that displays shades of pink, cream, and green.*

*The gray fur on the leaves of this peppermint geranium gives it a soft texture.*

*The fernlike leaves of sweet cicely* (Myrrhis odorata) *have a light, feathery texture.*

*The lacy, gray foliage of southernwood* (Artemisia abrotanum) *makes a delightful contrast to the wrinkled, bumpy texture of the tricolor sage* (Salvia officinalis 'Tricolor').

*Tansy's foliage is dark green and feathery.*

The textures of herbs can also delight the senses. Stroking the soft, furry leaves of lamb's-ears *(Stachys byzantina)* can be quite soothing. Some of the thymes, such as woolly thyme *(Thymus pseudolanuginosus),* also have a furry covering. And equally wonderful to touch are the velvety leaves of scented geraniums *(Pelargonium* spp.*),* lavender cotton *(Santolina chamaecyparissus),* and wormwood *(Artemisia absinthium).*

Other leaf textures offer visual excitement. Lemongrass *(Cymbopogon citratus)* is a beautiful ornamental grass that doubles as a delicious lemon flavoring for tea and a key ingredient in Asian, especially Thai, cooking. Its spiky leaf blades are slightly ridged, giving them a rough texture, but the overall form of the plant is a graceful fountain. A tender perennial, lemongrass is worth growing in a pot and bringing indoors for winter in cold climates.

Many varieties of sage have a fascinating crinkled, pebbly look. The leaves of borage (especially the older ones), comfrey *(Symphytum officinale),* and horehound *(Marrubium vulgare)* also have coarse, wrinkled textures due to a multitude of deep veins.

Feathery foliage abounds in the herb world. Coriander sends out horizontal strata of feathery leaves along its stem. Curly parsley is frilly and wavy. Fennel and dill produce masses of threadlike foliage, as does southernwood *(Artemisia abrotanum).* There is also the fernlike texture of yarrow, tansy, and rue or the lacy form of wormwood and chervil.

Lavender, rosemary, hyssop, and summer and winter savory all have short, narrow leaves, in some cases almost needlelike in appearance. Contrast these with the round or oval leaves of violets and some basils.

# Flower Forms and Colors

*The spiky purple blossoms of anise hyssop are as attractive in the flower bed as in the herb garden.*

*In autumn the pineapple-scented sage boasts brilliant scarlet flowers that are in striking contrast to its green leaves.*

The dazzling array of flower forms among herbs includes spiked and spired, star-shaped, cup-shaped, tubular, round-headed, and clustered types. Yarrow, for example, blooms in large, flat clusters that float on the top of long stems. Tansy flowers resemble little buttons, while scented geranium blossoms are small and delicate with five spread petals below and two overlapping above. Winter savory produces an abundance of small, tubular flowers along the stem, and clary sage sends out dramatic spikes of flowers. Lavender blossoms are tiny, but they cover the tip of the stalk, making a dramatic display. The light green flowers of angelica are large, umbrella-like clusters. To create visual interest and diversity in a flowering herb garden, combine flowers with different forms.

Most herb flowers are in the red or blue color family, running the gamut from pale pink and red, through lavender and purple, to blue. Among the most outstanding herbal flowers in this range are those of beebalm, which come in a variety of shades from soft pink to clear red. Or try catnip and catmint with white flowers; the pinkish purple flower heads of chives; pale pink, tubular comfrey flowers; pineapple-scented sage's brilliant scarlet blossoms; lavender-colored hyssop flowers; soft, lilac-colored mint blooms; the pale blue flowers of rosemary; white-, pink-, or lavender-flowered sage; pink-flowering thyme; sweet violets; and lavender. Also included in the family of herbs are foxgloves and pinks, both bearing striking pink blossoms.

*Other lovely flowering herbs are, clockwise from top left, valerian, borage, goldenrod, beebalm, and a creeping thyme* (Thymus praecox *'Coccineus'*).

*Beebalm produces an abundance of showy red, violet, pink, or white flowers throughout the summer. Shown here is 'Croftway Pink'.*

Herbs with bright yellow flowers include anise, fennel, tansy, rue, and santolina. Yarrow comes in yellow, white, and pink; nasturtium *(Tropaeolum majus)* in scarlet, yellow, and orange. Angelica and lady's-mantle blossoms are greenish yellow. Feverfew is a daisylike flower with bright yellow button centers surrounded by white petals. Coriander produces pure white (as well as pink) flower clusters, and some of the garlic flowers are white.

Use these and other lovely herb flowers to create dynamic color effects in your garden. Create a soothing view with the cool shades of blue, violet, and lavender, or opt for the dynamic, lively impact of warm reds and bright yellows.

You can use gray or silver foliage to soften a look or to tie together two contrasting colors. White flowers blend in easily with light colored ones. When combined with darker colors, white stands out in sharp contrast.

Experiment with different flower colors and forms, perhaps marrying a spiky blue flower with a round-headed yellow one. If you don't like the results, you can move the plants around in the fall or early spring. Finding the most appealing flower combinations is very much a matter of trial and error as well as one of personal taste—often the most pleasing grouping is reached purely by chance. Enjoy the process.

# A Culinary Herb Garden

**Plant List**

**1** Lemon thyme
*(Thymus × citriodorus)*
**2** Common thyme
*(Thymus vulgaris)*
**3** Creeping thyme
*(Thymus praecox)*
**4** Calendula
*(Calendula officinalis)*
**5** Nasturtium
*(Tropaeolum majus)*
**6** Tarragon
*(Artemisia dracunculus)*
**7** Chives
*(Allium schoenoprasum)*
**8** Chervil
*(Anthriscus cerefolium)*
**9** Summer and winter savory
*(Satureja hortensis,*
*S. montana)*
**10** Sage
*(Salvia officinalis)*
**11** Parsley
*(Petroselinum crispum)*
**12** Greek oregano
*(Origanum heracleoticum)*
**13** Rosemary
*(Rosmarinus officinalis)*
**14** Basil
*(Ocimum basilicum)*
**15** Bay
*(Laurus nobilis)*
**16** Fennel
*(Foeniculum vulgare)*
**17** Garlic chives
*(Allium tuberosum)*
**18** Dill
*(Anethum graveolens)*
**19** Salad burnet
*(Poterium sanguisorba)*

*F*or centuries cooks have used herbs to provide a gentle and healthful enrichment to the natural taste of the foods we eat. Due to climate and availability, different cultures feature different herbs in their cuisines. For example, Scandinavians use dill in many dishes, while Mexicans favor cilantro and oregano, and southern Europeans rely on basil, garlic, and oregano. Lemongrass is often a key ingredient in Thai cooking. American cuisine, as a "melting pot" of different culinary cultures, draws on a vast array of seasonings, many of which are grown in this appealing garden.

*Some herbs blend particularly well with certain foods. Here are some classic combinations—herbs and foods that just seem "right" together. Basil goes wonderfully with tomatoes and garlic; dill's sharp taste is softened by creamy or bland foods such as yogurt, sour cream, eggs, or potatoes; rosemary's strong piney flavor complements all meats; and tarragon adds an unusual, slightly sweet flavor to sauces, salad dressings, and delicate fish, chicken, and vegetable recipes. Try some of these time-honored marriages of food and herb flavors, but remember: experimenting with unusual combinations is part of the fun of cooking with herbs.*

# A Knot Garden

*The contrast in texture and color is one of the reasons this garden is so striking. Even though herbs are not generally considered colorful, the contrast of their foliage is surprisingly distinct and appealing when plants are grouped together and carefully maintained.*

*E*ven though knot gardens are reminiscent of the grand formal gardens of European palaces, they actually don't take a great deal of space to create. The secret to making a strong impact with a knot garden is to be very precise when laying out the plants and then to be diligent in keeping them trimmed back. Use the trimmings in crafts and in the kitchen.

**Plant List**
**1** Sage
*(Salvia officinalis)*
**2** Boxwood
*(Buxus sempervirens)*
**3** Germander
*(Teucrium chamaedrys)*
**4** Chives
*(Allium schoenoprasum)*
**5** Lavender cotton
*(Santolina chamaecyparissus)*
**6** Hyssop
*(Hyssopus officinalis)*
**7** Wormwood
*(Artemisia absinthium)*
**8** Creeping thyme
*(Thymus praecox)*
**9** Purple basil
*(Ocimum basilicum* 'Purpurascens' or 'Purple Ruffles'*)*

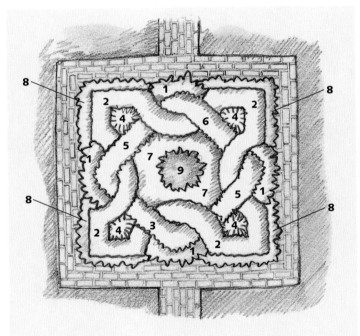

A brick pathway not only gives access to the garden, but also helps to define the shape. The brick path can also add design interest, as the bricks can be placed in different patterns and positions along the walkway. Another bonus is that mowing an adjacent lawn becomes much easier, as the wheel of the lawn mower can go right over the path, leaving an even edge.

# A Fragrance Garden

*Sit on the chamomile or thyme planters, and their fragrances will rise all around you. The planters are mulched with pine needles for their refreshing aroma. The cedar-block patio looks pretty and feels good on bare feet—and the blocks are resistant to weathering.*

A fragrance garden makes a wonderful sanctuary. Orient this garden so that the morning sun shines in from the open side: The trellis bearing hop vines will provide sweet-smelling relief from the afternoon sun. This garden surrounds you with invigorating and revitalizing scents. The lightly constructed trellis adds a decorative touch to this peaceful oasis and helps to hold the aromas in the area.

**Plant List**

**1** Chamomile
*(Chamaemelum nobile)*
**2** Pineapple-scented sage
*(Salvia elegans)*
**3** Thyme
*(Thymus vulgaris)*
**4** Rose geranium
*(Pelargonium graveolens)*
**5** English lavender
*(Lavandula angustifolia)*
**6** Rosemary
*(Rosmarinus officinalis)*
**7** Marjoram
*(Origanum majorana)*
**8** Sweet violet
*(Viola odorata)*
**9** Damask rose
*(Rosa damascena)*
**10** Hop
*(Humulus lupulus)*
**11** Catmint
*(Nepeta × faassenii)*
**12** Lemon balm
*(Melissa officinalis)*

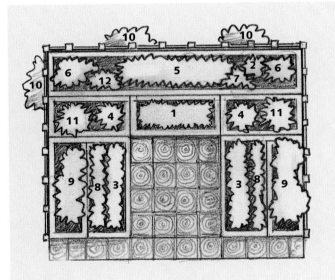

*The popularity of scented geraniums is well deserved. They are gregarious plants, mixing happily in the garden with one another or with other plants. They also make excellent container plants and can be moved indoors easily to spend the winter.*

*There are more than 200 species of scented geraniums available, including flowering types and ones with distinctive leaf shapes. Their aromas include rose, mint, apple, and nutmeg.*

# A Potpourri Garden

**Plant List**

**1** English lavender
(*Lavandula angustifolia*)
**2** Germander
(*Teucrium chamaedrys*)
**3** Apple geranium
(*Pelargonium
odoratissimum*)
**4** Costmary
(*Chrysanthemum balsamita*
var. *tanacetoides*)
**5** Beebalm
(*Monarda didyma*)
**6** Clary sage
(*Salvia sclarea*)
**7** Southernwood
(*Artemisia abrotanum*)
**8** Chamomile
(*Chamaemelum nobile*)
**9** Lemon verbena
(*Aloysia triphylla*)
**10** Orris
(*Iris × germanica* var.
*florentina*)
**11** Damask rose
(*Rosa damascena*)
**12** Rosemary
(*Rosmarinus officinalis*)
**13** Lavender cotton
(*Santolina chamaecyparissus*)
**14** Anise hyssop
(*Agastache foeniculum*)

*H*ere's a beautiful herb garden to look at and enjoy both during the growing season and afterward, when your herbal harvest allows you to create your own potpourri. A blend of fragrant flowers or a medley of herbs, flowers, and spices used to scent a room, potpourri is a lovely, long-lasting product of your work in the garden.

In addition to herbs, you will need essential oils, spices, and fixatives to make potpourri. Essential oils such as rose oil are expensive, but you need only a few drops and their essence lasts long after the herbs and flowers have lost their original scents. Fixatives are animal or vegetable substances that capture the essence of the oil and preserve its aroma for long periods of times. Once you have the basic ingredients, making a potpourri mixture lets you enjoy your herbs long after their first freshness.

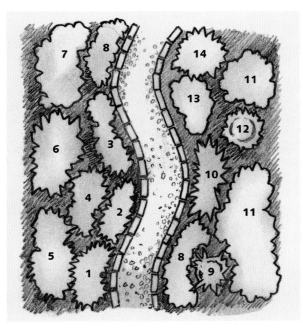

*One potpourri fixative that you can grow in your garden is orris (Iris × germanica var. florentina). To make the fixative, save a few rhizomes when you divide the plants, or dig up a few at the end of the growing season. Grind or chop the rhizomes, and store in the freezer until ready to use. You can also purchase powdered orrisroot from mail-order suppliers of herbs and potpourri ingredients.*

The gravel path is edged in brick to keep it neat, and the plantings are within arm's reach for easy harvesting.

The lemon verbena, a tender perennial, is already potted and can be brought indoors at the end of the season.

# Managing the Garden Environment

*P*lants grow in the wild without our care, but a plant struggling to exist under stressful conditions is not going to be as attractive or grow as well as one that is given an ideal environment. In your garden you can actively create a situation that allows plants to grow and flourish, reaching their full potential. • You can meet special environmental conditions for a wide variety of plants that normally would not be found together, mixing plants from different continents around the world. The resulting gardens can be beautiful, giving you great pleasure. • Managing the garden environment means providing good soil, adequate light, proper moisture, and even regulating the temperature with greenhouses and cold frames. A little care and effort to create good growing conditions for your plants will go a long way to making your garden successful.

# Soil Care

While it is true that many herbs have the constitution to tolerate poor soil conditions, all will grow more vigorously and be more beautiful if they are treated to a good-quality growing medium.

Unfortunately, poor soil is more common than good soil, and it is a lot of work and expense to transform a soil that is sandy or too heavy with clay into the ideally friable medium that allows plants to grow vigorously. However, the time and expense are long-term investments in the success of your garden. Before you plant, dig in enough compost and other organic material to give the soil a crumbly texture that allows it to drain well. For a garden devoted only to herbs, do not add manure or inorganic fertilizers. Fertilizers encourage soft, cold-sensitive growth that has little aroma. Once a bed is planted, add compost yearly as topdressing to maintain the soil's quality. Worms will mix the topdressing into the bed.

Many herbs, including lavender, winter savory, sage, marjoram, rosemary, and thyme, prefer an alkaline soil with a pH above 7.0. If your soil is acidic (pH below 6.5), add lime to raise the level if you want to grow these plants. Calcium carbonate is the easiest and safest form of lime to use. Ideally it should be dug in before planting. If that is not possible, apply it as a topdressing and then water to blend it in.

If you are preparing a bed for seeds, dig the soil, adding organic amendments. Remove any dirt clods and stones. Once the soil is well mixed, rake it in one direction. Sprinkle the seed, and then lightly rake at a 90-degree angle to cover the seed. Water lightly and keep moist until the seeds sprout.

*Although herbs can survive in poor soil, most will flourish and be more beautiful in a garden where the soil has been properly prepared.*

**1** *Before planting herbs, turn the soil to loosen it. Add compost and other organic material to make a crumbly mixture that drains well.*

**2** *Break up all dirt clods, crumbling them in your hands or crushing the larger clumps with your shovel.*

**3** *Collect and remove all stones and large pebbles that have come to the surface of the soil as a result of the digging.*

**4** *Rake the soil with a wide-tined rake to smooth and level it. Remove any new stones that surface.*

**5** *Use the back side of the rake, working in the opposite direction, to smooth the surface a second time and to create a finer soil consistency.*

# Light

### Herbs for Shade

*Most herbs prefer at least six hours of direct sunlight a day. If you have a shady or partially shady garden, however, don't despair. There are plenty of fragrant, tasty, and colorful herbs you can grow. Here is a selection of some herbs that can tolerate and even thrive in varying degrees of shade: angelica, chervil, chives, coltsfoot, costmary, foxglove, lady's-mantle, lemon balm, lovage, mint, parsley, sweet cicely, sweet flag, sweet woodruff, and tarragon. For the specific light requirements of each plant, consult the encyclopedia beginning on page 108.*

*This red-flowered cultivar of beebalm (Monarda didyma 'Cambridge Scarlet') grows in full sun or partial shade.*

*T*he issue of adequate light for plants can be confusing, especially when we see a plant known to need sun growing successfully in a shady area. The reason for the seeming contradiction is that there are many gradations and qualities of light. A bright, sunny day in a northern climate tends to be less intense than a bright day in the tropics. Similarly, a spot in the garden that is shady all day, but bright because of reflected light, may be better suited to plants than another corner that gets one or two hours of full sun a day, but is in dark shade the rest of the time.

Generally, when an herb is listed as requiring full sun, it needs a minimum of six hours of direct sunlight a day. If the plants get less sun, they tend to grow tall and scrawny while seeking the sun, and their flavor diminishes.

Most herbs prefer plenty of sunlight. Many of the most popular herbs, such as oregano, marjoram, and sage, come from the Mediterranean, where they enjoy hot days and lots of sun in a free-draining soil. Nevertheless, there are exceptions. Herbs such as horseradish, lemon balm, and lovage can grow in sun or partial shade. In these cases, partial shade means a spot that gets less than six hours of direct sun a day, but is fairly bright. Other herbs, such as mints, marsh mallow, and angelica, will thrive in full shade.

# Moisture

## Herbs for Moist Conditions

*Most herbs do best in hot, dry, sunny conditions with well-drained soil. These herbs prefer, or at least tolerate, wetter conditions: angelica, comfrey, foxglove, horsetail, lady's-mantle, lovage, marsh mallow, mint, pennyroyal, sorrel, sweet flag, sweet woodruff, valerian, and violets.*

*Lady's-mantle* (Alchemilla mollis), *with its yellow-green flowers and bushy gray-green leaves, is an ideal herb to plant if you have wet conditions in your garden.*

Gardeners can keep quite busy looking for ways to provide and maintain moisture to the plants—encouraging deep roots by slow watering that soaks in deeply, mulching heavily and frequently, or using drip irrigation and other techniques. In contrast, most herbs prefer a dry environment, and some, such as thyme, will rot if they get too wet for too long.

In dry climates it's easy to allow the herbs to dry out between watering, but in rainy areas it's essential that the soil drain readily. Sandy or slightly gravelly soil is ideal for many types of herbs. If your soil is heavy with clay and drains slowly, you can improve it by adding organic amendments as recommended on page 54. Working in compost or peat moss will be an improvement; so will sawdust, old plaster, leaves, and ashes. The goal is to break up the fine, tightly packed soil particles to let in air and enhance drainage. Once you've done your major soil makeover, your program of soil amendment should be ongoing. Experienced gardeners live by the adage that you never put a spade into the ground without adding compost or other amendments.

If digging and improving the soil to increase drainage sounds like too much backbreaking work, you can avoid the problem by creating raised beds. In addition to solving drainage problems, raised beds bring the plants closer to eye level and break the monotony of a horizontal garden. A raised bed can be

# *Moisture* CONTINUED

as simple as a mound of topsoil held in place with edging plants such as lavender, or as elaborate as a planter made of stone, brick, wood, or cement. Shallow-rooted herbs need as little as 6 to 8 inches of root room, although if you raise your bed a foot or two, it is easier to reach for tending and harvesting, and you can sit on the rim while you work. Be sure the beds are narrow enough so that you can comfortably reach halfway across to tend the plants. If the raised bed is solidly enclosed with brick or cement, be sure to fill it with a well-drained soil mix, or you may undo all your good work by drowning your plants. You may also want to put down a layer of sand or gravel at the bottom of the raised bed before adding topsoil.

A sloped area, even if the soil is heavy, has better drainage than level ground because the water constantly runs off, rather than accumulating. Sweet woodruff *(Galium odoratum)* is an excellent ground cover on shady hillsides, and different varieties of creeping thyme are spectacular in sunny situations. Or you could fill a sunny hillside with different herb plants to create an informal, cottage-style herb garden. Pack them in closely to keep down the weeds, and place stepping-stones into the hillside in a meandering path so that you can walk among the plants to enjoy the scents and to harvest the leaves.

If your herb garden is in a low-lying area where water accumulates, you will need to build drains. The easiest solution is to contour the land so that all the water runs off into a gully or ditch. To make the drain more attractive, fill it with river stones or smaller pebbles, creating a dry "river." More complicated solutions include installing drainage pipes or creating French drains, which are deep ditches filled with several inches of gravel and then topped with soil.

*Generally, gray-leaved plants prefer dry conditions. Here gray lavender cotton (Santolina chamaecyparissus) is planted with its cousin, the green-leaved Santolina virens. Growing behind them are rosemary and lavender, both of which do well in hot, dry climates.*

Not all herbs, however, require dry soil. If you believe in taking the course of least resistance, then plant herbs that can tolerate damp conditions. In addition to the plants that prefer damp soil listed in the sidebar on page 57, there is quite a long list of possibilities that will adapt to average or moist circumstances. If your soil is moist but not waterlogged, try calendula *(C. officinalis)*, chamomile *(Chamaemelum nobile)*, chervil *(Anthriscus cerefolium)*, chives *(Allium schoenoprasum)*, clary sage *(Salvia sclarea)*, dill *(Anethum graveolens)*, fennel *(Foeniculum vulgare)*, garlic *(Allium sativum)*, horseradish *(Armoracia rusticana)*, lemon balm *(Melissa officinalis)*, lemongrass *(Cymbopogon citratus)*, lemon verbena *(Aloysia triphylla)*, rue *(Ruta graveolens)*, saffron *(Crocus sativus)*, summer and winter savory *(Satureja hortensis* and *S. montana)*, sweet cicely *(Myrrhis odorata)*, tansy *(Tanacetum vulgare)*, and wintergreen *(Gaultheria procumbens)*.

If you hanker for a marsh or bog garden that includes herbs, but don't have a wet-enough space on your property, you can create the conditions yourself. Dig out the soil from the area you want to make boggy, creating a hole about 1 foot deep and as wide and long as you want. Line the hole with heavy plastic, then refill with the soil and water heavily. You may need to water during long dry spells. In addition to herbs, attractive bog plants include Japanese and pseudacorus irises, primulas, lobelias, astilbes, hostas, and daylilies.

If you live in a very dry region such as the Southwest, where it may not rain for eight or nine months, even drought-tolerant herbs will need some irrigation. Besides hand watering with a hose or watering can, your options for different systems include sprinklers, drip irrigation, and soaker hoses.

Both drip irrigation and soaker hoses operate on a low-pressure system that delivers the water directly to the root zone at a rate as slow as half a gallon per hour. They are better than the old-fashioned sprinkler systems for most garden applications, except lawns, because the leaves of the plants stay dry. (When leaves get wet, they are more susceptible to disease and sunburn.) In addition, with a slow-delivery system you have less runoff. The water can soak in deeply where it's needed, permeating right down to the lowest roots. These two methods of watering also reduce weeds since water is directed exactly where it's needed, and the surrounding soil, which may harbor weed seeds, is left dry.

A valuable accessory to any sprinkler system is a timer that turns the water on and off automatically according to a preprogrammed schedule. Timers are now so refined they can be set to run for just seconds or for as long as hours. Since most mechanical timers cannot be set to turn on for more than an hour, a drip system, which often needs to run for several hours at a time to disperse enough water, requires an electronic timer. Among the obvious benefits of timers is that you are free to leave home for weeks without worrying about your garden withering away in your absence. You may want to ask a friend or neighbor to check on your garden to make sure your timers are working properly, however.

**Drought-Tolerant Herbs**
*As a general rule, herbs originating in the Mediterranean are drought tolerant. Plants with gray foliage also tend to prefer dry conditions. Consider these herbs for dry places: borage, chives, fennel, feverfew, germander, lavender, Roman chamomile, rosemary, sage, savory, southernwood, thyme, wormwood, and yarrow.*

# Temperature Considerations

*J*ust like other types of plants, herbs have varying tolerances and preferences in regard to temperature. Many of the perennials are quite hardy and will grow where winter temperatures dip below −20°F. Beebalm, betony, catnip, costmary, horehound, hyssop, rue, Roman chamomile, sage, southernwood, tansy, tarragon, valerian, wintergreen, and wormwood are all fairly hardy. (For more details on each plant's hardiness, see the Encyclopedia of Plants beginning on page 108.) Chives, elecampane, lovage, mugwort, sweet cicely, sweet flag, and sweet woodruff are even hardier, growing as far north as zone 4. And yarrow will even sometimes tolerate zone 2 winters. All these plants are good choices for northern herb gardens. The Mediterranean herbs, including thyme, oregano, marjoram, and lavender, can withstand a good deal of heat in summer.

### ▼ Cool Climates

Some herbs are tender perennials that cannot survive northern winters. Indigo and scented geraniums cannot stand freezing temperatures at all and will winter over only in zones 10 and 11. Lemon verbena and sweet marjoram are perennial to zone 9, and bay and rosemary to zone 8. Unless you live where these plants are hardy, you must grow them as annuals, starting with new plants each spring, or in pots that you bring indoors over winter. See the Encyclopedia of Plants section beginning on page 108 for details on handling individual plants.

There are annual herbs, too, and they are treated like annual flowers. Hardy annuals such as calendula, chervil, coriander, dill, and German chamomile (*Matricaria recutita*) can tolerate some light frost, and their seeds will survive winter conditions in much of the United States. They can be sown in fall in many gardens to give them an early start the following spring, or you can sow or transplant them outdoors in spring when the danger of heavy frost is past but an occasional light frost is still possible. Tender annuals such as basil, on the other hand, cannot go into the garden until all danger of frost is past and the soil has warmed.

### ▼ Warm Climates

In frost-free climates, you can grow most perennials—and even annuals—for year-round harvesting. The few perennial exceptions are tarragon (*Artemisia dracunculus)* and other members of the artemisia family, including southernwood (*A. abrotanum*), Roman wormwood (*A. pontica*), and silver mound (*A. schmidtiana* 'Nana'), which all go dormant in the winter, dying back to their roots.

To keep a continuous supply of the annual herbs growing, simply sow new seeds whenever the old plant begins to wear out or get too woody. Since seeds germinate best when the soil is warm, during the cooler winter months start the seeds indoors, following the procedures for starting seed on pages 64–67. You don't have to wait until the last frost date to begin moving the newly started seeds outside. As soon as the plants have a few sets of mature leaves, begin the hardening-off process, and then plant them in the ground. The exception is basil, which needs a truly warm environment to grow and flourish. Unless you live in an area with very mild winters, such as along the coast in southern California, don't waste your time trying to grow basil out of season.

Even "frost-free" climates get the occasional fluke cold snap when temperatures drop below freezing. Some annuals may even survive such conditions, depending on how cold sensitive they are and how

Native to tropical regions, the fountainlike lemongrass (Cymbopogon citratus) *is a delightful addition to temperate gardens. Its lemony leaves are excellent for flavoring soup or tea.*

## Herbs to Bring Indoors for Winter

*If you live where winters are cold, you can grow bay, lemongrass, lemon verbena, rosemary, and scented geraniums in pots and bring them indoors during winter.*

*Although they may not last the winter, try planting the following in pots and bringing them indoors to a sunny windowsill before frost to continue the harvest of fresh leaves for another month or so: basil, chervil, chives, coriander, dill, marjoram, oregano, parsley, and thyme.*

many hours the frost persists. Expect to lose basil, perilla, and cumin to these rare frosty days unless you take measures to protect them. If the plants are valuable to you and you are warned about the coming cold, cover them with a blanket, box, or bushel basket to keep them warm.

Among the annual herbs that can take light frost are anise, borage, calendula, chervil, coriander, dill, German chamomile, and summer savory. Grow them throughout the year in warm climates. In cold-winter climates, these can be planted outside early in spring before the last guaranteed frost date or even sown in autumn to be overwintered indoors.

Tender perennials, such as some mints, lavender, rosemary, and lemon verbena, also can take mild frost, but they may suffer some die-back. If they do get singed by the cold, wait until warmer weather to prune away the dead parts. Although unsightly, they give the plant some protection during future freezes. When you see new growth appearing, cut away the damaged tops. As with the annuals, in mild areas where frost is rare, you can cover these vulnerable plants when the weather predictions are severely cold to try to save them, or accept the loss philosophically. After all, most of the country cannot garden at all, except for indoors, during the winter months.

# CHAPTER 3

# Growing Herbs

*a*s any herb aficionado will tell you, herbs are among the most satisfying plants to grow. They don't require much maintenance and are forgiving of neglect. Some herbs are reputed to improve the vigor and flavor of vegetables growing nearby; others are valued because they discourage insect pests and plant diseases. • Besides being easy to grow, most herbs are also easy to propagate. Many grow readily from seed, while others will root from cuttings in a matter of weeks. Others are so generous in their growth habits that many new plants can be divided from a parent plant. • Herbs are versatile, too, adapting to pots or the garden, growing satisfactorily both indoors and out.

# Starting Seeds Indoors

## Herbs That Are Difficult to Start from Seed

*Most herbs will grow easily from seed, germinating within a matter of days or a week or two. However, the following herbs are tricky to grow from seed and are best purchased as plants or propagated vegetatively.*

*Angelica seed loses its viability quickly. Cumin requires at least three months of high temperatures. Lavender, lavender cotton, lemon balm, lemongrass, lemon verbena, mint, rosemary, southernwood, sweet woodruff, thyme, winter savory, and wormwood germinate very slowly. Parsley is erratic in its germination, and tarragon produces sterile seeds.*

Starting seeds indoors six to eight weeks before the last frost date in your region is a good way to get a jump on your spring garden, especially for annual herbs, such as basil, that are a mainstay in the summer kitchen. Many people expect it to be a lot of work. In fact, once your supplies are collected, it takes only a few minutes to sow the seed—then just let nature take care of the rest for you.

To start seeds indoors, the only supplies you need are clean planting containers, a sterile potting mix, and the seeds. Seeds can be planted in all sorts of clean recycled containers such as yogurt or plastic cups, egg cartons, or last year's cell packs from the nursery. Poke holes in the bottom of these containers, and then keep them on a tray to catch the runoff water. If you plan to plant a lot of seeds, it will be easier to purchase commercial seed-starting containers. These plastic seed trays have three components: a planting tray that has holes for drainage, a liner to hold the excess water that drains off, and a clear plastic, domed lid to maintain moisture while the seeds are sprouting. A 10-by-20-inch tray will hold 98 plants in cells that are about 1½ inches square.

Your local nursery should carry bags of potting mix meant for starting seeds. This is a specially prepared mixture that is very light, making it easy for seeds to sprout and quickly grow good root systems. The packages recommend adding different amounts of water to the soil while it's still in the bag, depending on the size of the bag. It's an easy, no-mess way to wet the soil just the right amount without turning it to slush. Once your potting soil is properly moistened, spoon it into your container, and tamp it down gently to remove excess air.

There are some herbs that are very difficult to grow from seed (see the sidebar on this page). Some seeds

**1** *To sow herb seeds indoors, first fill the bottom of the pot with a ½-inch layer of gravel or perlite to promote good drainage.*

**4** *For reliable germinators, plant three seeds per pot. For reluctant sprouters, such as lavender, plant as many as a dozen seeds.*

**2** Fill the pot with moist soil. Use a good-quality potting mix with a light texture so that the seeds will easily sprout in the container.

**3** Tamp down the soil with your hands and level it, leaving about ½-inch space from the top of the pot to allow room for watering.

**5** Label each pot with the seed variety and the date you planted them. This will help you identify look-alike seedlings later.

**6** Cover the pot with a plastic bag to create a miniature greenhouse that will retain moisture until the seeds sprout. Place the pot in a warm spot.

# Starting Seeds Indoors CONTINUED

**1** As soon as seeds sown indoors sprout, remove the plastic cover from the pot so that air can circulate. Give the plants adequate light.

**2** Using a mist spray, keep the plants moist until they are 2 inches tall, then allow the surface to dry between waterings.

**3** Thin your seedlings by cutting off the tops of the less-healthy-looking specimens. This will give healthier seedlings more room to grow.

germinate erratically, meaning that you'll get very few plants from a packet of seeds. Others are extremely slow to sprout, and still others, such as tarragon, produce sterile seeds. Another group of herbs do better if they are sown directly into the soil rather than started indoors in pots (see the sidebar on page 70). These may have long taproots or be sensitive to being transplanted. It's important to be aware which herbs are not suited to starting early from seed.

When the containers are ready, plant the seeds, following the directions on the packet about the recommended depth. Some small seeds simply need to be set on top of the soil and lightly pressed in. Others require a planting depth of ⅛ to ¼ inch, so that they can germinate in darkness. In those cases, you may want to use a pencil to create the small hole.

Once your seeds are planted, cover the container with clear plastic bags (or the plastic domed tops if you are using commercial seed trays) to keep in the moisture and warmth. By doing this you are creating a miniature greenhouse environment for the seeds. Now wait for the seeds to germinate. Most of the herb seeds should sprout in a week to 10 days. The seed packet will indicate how long to expect for each variety. Once the seeds sprout, remove the plastic covering to allow air to circulate. If you don't, you are likely to lose your entire collection of seedlings to a complex of fungi known as damping-off.

At this point your seedlings need a lot of light—at least 12 hours a day. If they don't get enough light they are liable to get thin and leggy. If you use artificial light, opt for fluorescent or growing lights, rather than incandescent, and keep them about a foot from

*Before you transplant seedlings started indoors into the garden, harden them off by setting them outside each day for a week or two. Begin with less than an hour, and gradually increase the amount of time left outside.*

the top of the plants. Incandescent lights can get too hot, and they don't generate the ultraviolet light plants require. If you have a good, sunny windowsill, use that for growing seedlings, but turn the plants every four days so that they get even exposure.

To keep the soil moist without damaging the fragile plants, mist with water daily, or set the seedling containers on several layers of wet newspaper, which will work as a capillary mat. The water will be absorbed through the drainage holes in the bottom of the container. Every two weeks, feed the seedlings with a weak solution of liquid fertilizer, diluted to half the recommended strength.

The odds are that your seedlings will be growing too close together for comfort. If you can, prick out some and move them to other containers. Always handle the tiny, delicate seedlings by their leaves, not the stems, which are too easy to break. Otherwise, snip off the less-healthy-looking specimens with nail scissors to give ample growing space to the more vigorous ones.

Your last act of care before transplanting outside is to prepare the young plants for the transition from a protected environment to the harsher outdoor conditions. This process is called hardening off. About two weeks before you transplant, take your seedlings outside for less than an hour. Each day increase their time outside by 30 minutes until you are ready to make the transition permanent, in about two weeks.

Starting seeds indoors is certainly more work than a quick trip to the nursery for bedding plants, but the rewards are many. Besides saving money, it's an opportunity to enjoy the touch and smell of growing things early in the season.

# Planting Outdoors

Once the weather warms up, it's time to take your herb garden outdoors. In mild regions that may be as early as February. Spring comes much later in colder places. Wait until the published last frost date for your area, or a couple of weeks later, before you take tender annuals outside. Before planting homegrown seedlings outdoors, harden them off as described on page 67.

If you planted your seeds in large, undivided flats, use an old kitchen knife or your trowel to cut the soil around each plant, as if you were slicing pieces of sheet cake. Gently lift out each plant, being careful to keep the cube of soil around the roots. The less the roots are disturbed, the faster the young plant will establish itself in its new growing site. Plant immediately, keeping the soil level the same as it was in the flats, and water well.

If there are too many seedlings in the undivided flat to cut around each one, then you must prick out each one. Use a pencil or similar object to gently uproot individual plants. Some soil may cling to the root, but often it will come up bare. Plant each tiny seedling immediately. Be careful when you water that the flow doesn't wash the plants away altogether or splash earth onto them. Wet soil can prevent the sun from reaching the leaves, or even bury the small plants completely. You will need to water these tiny plants frequently until the roots have grown.

Peat pots are a wonderful recent development. As their name suggests, they are made of peat, an important component of rich, well-drained soil. Herbs grown in peat pots can be planted, pot and all, directly into the garden. Not only is this easy for you, but the plant benefits by not having its roots disturbed.

*These rooted cuttings and seedlings growing in 1-inch containers will reach their mature size by the end of the summer if they are transplanted outdoors into a favorable growing situation.*

**1** When transplanting seedlings outdoors, prepare the garden bed and amend the soil as you would for any new plants.

**2** With a small trowel, dig your planting holes. Be sure to make each hole a little bigger than the plant's root ball.

**3** Fill each hole with water, and allow it to drain completely. If drainage is slow, add soil amendments.

**4** Gently remove seedlings from their pot. Be careful to keep the entire root ball and attached soil intact.

**5** Place each plant in its hole and cover the roots with soil. Press down firmly to remove any air pockets.

**6** Water the plants well. Be sure to use a fairly fine spray so that you don't wash away the soil or uproot the plant.

# *Planting Outdoors* CONTINUED

**Seeds to Sow Directly into the Ground**

*These herbs do not transplant well and are best sown directly in the garden where you want the plants to grow: anise, chervil, coriander, dill, fennel, Roman chamomile, and summer savory.*

Eventually the roots will grow right through the pot, which will break up into the soil. Be sure to tear away the portion of the peat pot that is above the soil line. Otherwise the exposed rim will act as a wick, drawing water out of the soil and away from the plants. You may also tear the sides of the pot to make it easier for roots to grow through.

It can be slightly tricky to extract seedlings growing in plastic cell packs or individual plastic containers. Gently squeeze the sides of the container to loosen the soil and roots from the edge. Then put two fingers along the sides of the plant's stem to support it, and turn the container upside down. If the plant doesn't slide out into your hand, pull the stem gently with your fingers, squeezing the sides of the container at the same time. Before you plant, check the root ball. Nursery-grown plants may be root-bound. If the roots are growing in a tight tangle all along the edge or at the bottom of the root ball, tear away some of the outer roots and split the root ball an inch or two from the bottom. That rough treatment will encourage the plant to produce new feeder roots that will extend out into the garden soil.

Herbs purchased from the nursery in quart and gallon containers should be handled in much the same way as those sold in the little 2- and 3-inch pots, including loosening up coiled, tight roots. However, since the root ball is much bigger, you should take more care in digging your hole. Dig the planting hole wider and deeper than the container, and if your soil isn't of good quality, amend the soil from the hole you dug with organic matter to make it lighter and looser. Fill the hole with water and allow it to drain away. Then return a few inches of the amended soil to the hole so that the base of the plant is level with the ground. Place the plant in the hole, and fill in the gaps with the extra soil. Tamp down the soil firmly to remove any air gaps, then water again.

Some herbs fare better if they are sown directly into the ground, rather than started early in pots indoors. The most common reasons for their sensitivity are a long taproot, general dislike of being transplanted, or both. Most herbs that need to be seeded directly into the garden should be planted in early spring, as soon as the soil is ready to work. A few, such as catnip, chervil, and fennel, can also be sown in autumn.

Succession planting, or a frequent sowing of seeds, will keep some herbs plentiful all season. Dill, for example, is grown both for its seeds and its foliage. The leaves have the fullest flavor before the flower heads open; however, if you remove the flowers, you lose the seeds. The solution is succession planting. Since it is an annual herb, dill will grow to maturity fairly quickly. Plant seeds every few weeks through August, and you will have fresh foliage as well as maturing seeds throughout the season. Other good herbs for succession planting are chervil, coriander, and parsley.

Before you plant seeds directly outdoors, be sure to prepare your soil, adding amendments to make it loose and friable. Follow the packet instructions about spacing and depth. Once a seed is planted and watered, it must be kept moist at all times or it will shrivel and die. After the seed has germinated and grown a bit, the expanding roots will seek moisture deeper in the soil, so you don't need to water as frequently.

Most herbs need a bit of extra tender care when they are first transplanted. Water them regularly for several weeks until the roots have a chance to spread.

**TROUBLESHOOTING TIP**

*When sowing seeds outdoors, it's very hard to see where the seeds have fallen, especially if they are small and brown, matching the color of the soil. If you are planting rows of seeds, run a strip of toilet paper down the furrow and plant the seeds on top. That way, you can see exactly where each seed is, and the buried paper will quickly break down into the soil. Mix tiny seeds with sand, and disperse them with a salt shaker.*

**1** *To transplant a large plant into the garden, tap the bottom of the pot with your hand or a trowel in order to loosen the soil. Slide the plant out carefully.*

**2** *If the roots are twisted and have outgrown the pot, loosen them carefully before putting the plant into the ground.*

**3** *Fill the planting hole with water, let it drain, and then place the plant so that the root ball is just below the surface of the soil.*

**4** *Sprinkle the water slowly and deeply, making sure it soaks into the soil to moisten the plant's roots completely. Water as needed to keep the plant moist.*

# Planting Invasive Herbs

While it is a struggle to get some plants to grow, others are invasive once they are established. Most infamous for its encroaching qualities in the herb family is mint, but horseradish, tarragon, sweet woodruff, and several other herbs can also become invasive because of underground rhizomes that spread or prolific self-sowing.

The best way to control mint is to keep it in a pot. If you want it to look as if it were growing in the garden, bury the container. Mint has been known to jump a container, but it's harder to do than spreading freely in the ground. Other ideas are to plant mint in flue tiles buried to the rim or in bottomless wooden boxes with 1-foot-high sides. The metal strips used for edging beds generally are too shallow to do much good to prevent spreading. Horseradish and tarragon also are good candidates to curtail in a container.

Other plants that spread by underground rhizomes or roots include tansy, beebalm, costmary, violets, lemon balm (a member of the mint family), and mugwort *(Artemisia vulgaris)*. Either give them a lot of room to spread, or be prepared to divide them frequently. Violets will bloom better if they are divided every year. Either split and replant the divisions, or just detach the runners. In addition to dividing lemon balm, prune the plant to help contain it.

Among the prolific self-sowers are perilla, catnip, mugwort, lemon balm, and fennel. Left to its own devices, fennel will naturalize in empty lots and along the roadside in climates suited to its needs. If that's a problem, control the seeds by removing the flower heads before the seeds have a chance to ripen.

*Most of the hundreds of mint varieties, including the apple mint shown here, spread rapidly, becoming invasive if not properly contained.*

# Planting in Containers

Whether they are growing indoors or outside, many herbs do beautifully in containers. Shallow-rooted herbs useful in the kitchen, such as chives, thyme, basil, summer savory, sage, and even scented geraniums, can live on a sunny kitchen windowsill in pots as small as 6 inches, at least for a few months. If the plants outgrow their pots, either transplant them to 8-inch pots or, if appropriate, divide the plant and replant the divisions in small pots.

The sweet bay or laurel *(Laurus nobilis)*, the source of the bay leaves so indispensable in cooking, can grow to be a 50-foot tree in a suitable location, but you can keep it as small as 2 feet with frequent shearing. Bay adapts well to a 12-inch container and can even be pruned as a topiary with a symmetrical, round head atop a straight trunk. This tender tree is hardy only to zone 8, but in colder climates a potted specimen can be brought inside for winter and kept in a cool, well-lit spot. A tidy evergreen, the sweet bay is an asset both indoors and out.

Other herbs that benefit from 12-inch or larger pots include tarragon, winter savory, and upright rosemary. Parsley has a taproot and needs a pot at least 8 inches deep. Dill can be grown in a pot, but it dislikes being transplanted, so you are wise to start it from seed.

Herbs that sprawl and spread are ideal for hanging baskets, where they can arch down in a pretty cascade. Mint, prostrate rosemary, and oregano are three good candidates. You can also plant them on the edges of large pots or in the front of a window box, where they can drape their stems over the sides. Plant an upright herb, such as catnip, in the center of the pot to create a striking bouquet. Use creeping ground-cover herbs such as thyme and chamomile to cover exposed soil in any pot arrangement.

Regardless of the herbs you choose to put in your pots, the first thing that must go in is soil. Since growing in a container is slightly more stressful for the plant than growing in the garden, you want to provide the best possible growing medium. Good drainage is absolutely essential for herbs growing in containers. Whether you blend your own potting mix or buy a packaged mix, it must drain quickly while still retaining sufficient moisture for plant roots.

One good potting medium that you can mix yourself for growing herbs contains equal parts of good garden loam (or you can use topsoil or packaged potting soil), crumbled compost (or leaf mold or composted livestock manure), peat moss, and perlite or vermiculite. Mix all the ingredients thoroughly. If you use packaged potting soil for the soil component, read the label to make sure it is all soil and not a peat-based planting mix, which may be called "potting soil" on the bag.

Instead of blending your own potting medium, you can use a commercially prepared mix, choosing from soil-based and peat-based mixes. The soil-based mixes contain more nutrients and dry out less quickly. It is a good idea to add some perlite or vermiculite to this type of mix to be sure of good drainage. The peat-based products are lighter in weight, but they dry out rapidly and must never be allowed to dry out completely. Plants in a peat-based potting mix will need frequent watering, especially in hot, windy weather.

Whether you choose a soil- or peat-based mix, be prepared to fertilize your potted herbs. In the ground most herbs are more flavorful and aromatic when they are not fed. However, the natural nutrients in potted soil leach out very quickly because of frequent watering, so herbs in containers do need regular feeding. The exact timing for fertilizing depends on the

# *Planting in Containers* CONTINUED

herbs you are growing, how often you water, and the ingredients of the planting mix. The more often you water, the more frequently you should fertilize. A peat moss and perlite planting mix should be fertilized more often than one that contains vermiculite. (Although vermiculite contains no nutrients, it does absorb moisture and thus needs watering less often than perlite.) Watch the condition of your plants, and make your own judgment.

Even drought-tolerant herbs need to be watered more often in containers than when planted in the ground. On very hot days, small containers outdoors may need to be watered as often as twice daily. However, there are tricks to preserve moisture in pots, which are especially valuable in extremely hot, dry climates and for people who need be away for a few days at a stretch.

Unless you are growing a plant that performs better when root-bound, choose a large pot. The plant will need less water because there is more soil around the roots to keep damp. Plastic containers hold moisture best, followed in order of efficiency by metal, concrete, glazed ceramic, wood, and clay. If you don't like the look of a plastic or metal pot, slip it inside a more attractive clay, wood, or ceramic container. If possible, choose white containers because they reflect the heat, reducing moisture loss. Keep your containers out of drying wind, and group the containers together so that they can shade and humidify each other. Mulch the soil in your pots with 1 or 2 inches of organic matter or compost. A layer of dry grass clippings works well. Top that with bark for a neat, attractive look.

Slip potted herbs into a basket for a charming table centerpiece.

Hardy only in zones 8–10, society garlic (Tulbaghia violacea) is perfect for a container that can be brought indoors during winter.

A variety of scented geraniums make an attractive display in a long wooden planter. Containers look prettiest when bursting with flowers.

Lifted off the ground and placed in a pot rack, this parsley stays clean and is easy to harvest.

Be creative in choosing containers for your herbs. These colorful tins add a delightful bit of whimsy to this garden.

A decorative clay pot gives a dash of color and verve to this garden spot.

# Planting in Containers CONTINUED

**EARTH · WISE TIP**

Soil polymers are a fairly new product designed to help soil maintain moisture. They are especially valuable in very dry climates and for containers that dry out much faster than ground soil. Mix the polymers with the potting soil in the recommended proportions. You will still need to water your pots more frequently than the rest of the garden, but the polymers will help the soil retain moisture longer.

**1** Line the bottom of the window box with broken clay pots or gravel for drainage.

**2** Fill the planter with a good-quality soil or a packaged potting mix.

**5** Attach support brackets beneath the window at a height that will bring the box to the level of the window.

**6** Attach the window box to the brackets, making sure to center the planter below the window.

**3** Arrange the herbs you wish to plant in the box so that they look attractive.

**4** Plant the herbs, allowing enough space between them so that they can grow to their full size.

TROUBLESHOOTING TIP

*Grow herbs with cascading habits, such as prostrate rosemary and creeping thyme, in hanging baskets. Hang them from the eaves in a southern-facing location or from a tree branch. Make sure the plants get enough direct sun—at least six hours a day—and be watchful of their water needs.*

**7** Water window boxes regularly so that they don't dry out, and fertilize monthly once the plants are established.

# Caring for Herbs

*H*erbs are among the most care-free plants. However, they do need some attention to keep them growing vigorously and looking their best.

Keep your garden free of weeds. Weeds not only make the garden look untidy, they rob nearby plants of water and nutrients, and they can harbor disease and pests. Weeds are easiest to pull in the spring, when they are young and have shallow roots. Most important, be sure to remove weeds from the garden before they set seed. If you catch the weeds when they are very tiny, you can disturb the roots enough to kill or at least weaken them by simply cultivating the ground. Otherwise your best approach is to pull them out individually, roots and all. If you are removing a weed with a long taproot, such as dandelion, dig, rather than pull it, so that you can remove the entire taproot. The task may be hard on your back and

**1** *Cultivate the soil around your plants with a hoe or single-pronged garden fork to keep down weeds, aerate the soil, and avoid compaction.*

knees, but you do gain a sense of accomplishment. Fortunately, a number of weeding tools are available to make the job easier.

During the hot summer months, you may need to water your herbs occasionally if there is not adequate rainfall. How often the plants need irrigating depends on the kind of soil in which they're growing (water pours right through sandy soil, so it dries out faster), the water requirements of individual plants (once established, for example, rosemary needs no extra irrigation except in desert regions), and the frequency and amount of rain.

Herbs growing in pots will need to be watered regularly, depending on the plants and whether the pots get full sun all day or some shade. Don't rely solely on rain to provide enough water for potted plants. Because the foliage covers most of the soil in pots, even a heavy rainfall will barely moisten the soil in most containers. Also, as explained on pages 73–74, herbs growing in pots do need an occasional light fertilizer, in contrast to herbs growing in the ground, where feeding tends to encourage leggy growth, dissipating the plant's natural flavor and aroma.

Herbs are generally pest-free, although Japanese beetles can sometimes be a problem, feeding on many ornamentals in addition to herbs. You can catch the iridescent beetles in specially designed traps baited with a sweet scent. But if you use traps, place them well away from the garden, or they may attract additional beetles from all over the neighborhood to your garden instead of reducing your local population. If the infestation is small, handpick the pests and either crush them or drown them in soapy water (the squeamish should wear gloves). If all else fails, you can use

*Some flowering herbs, such as this feathery, tall-growing dill, will self-sow prolifically if the ripe seeds are not harvested.*

a pesticide spray, but handle any pesticide—even an organic one—with extreme caution. It's best to avoid them on herbs grown for kitchen use.

Once you have a problem with Japanese beetles, the most effective approach to eliminating them is to kill their young larvae (white grubs with brown or orange heads that live in lawns, causing them much damage as well). You can spray the lawn with the poison Diazinon or opt for a biological control developed in 1933. Researchers found that the bacteria called milky spore *(Bacillus popilliae)* killed 90 percent of the Japanese beetle larvae in lawns in a two-month period. Once the disease is established (which takes a couple of years), it will spread on its own. The decaying bodies of diseased grubs release the bacteria back into the soil, where they are picked up by other larvae. Milky spore, in powder form, is available at most nurseries.

Just as houses benefit from spring cleaning, gardens need a fall cleanup. Rake away leaves and pull out spent annual plants. If you plan to take any herbs indoors for winter, begin readying them for the change of environment (see the section on preparing for winter on pages 91–93).

# Companion Planting with Herbs

Companion planting is an environmentally friendly way of controlling pests and diseases and promoting symbiotic relationships with plants. For reasons not fully understood, certain plants are thought to grow better when planted near each other, while other plants appear to discourage or repel pests. It is believed that root secretions and plant odors are factors. When plants are grown together to enhance growth or repel pests, it is called companion planting.

A lot of herbs are believed to have beneficial properties when grown near other plants. For example, chamomile *(Chamaemelum nobile)* is reputed to keep all nearby plants healthy. Planted around fruit trees, garlic *(Allium sativum)* is thought to protect against borers; near tomatoes, to discourage red spider mites; and near roses, to repel aphids. On the other hand, all plants in the *Allium* genus are said to slow the growth of peas and beans.

Chamomile and sage *(Salvia)* marry well with plants from the cabbage, or cole, family. Sage repels the white cabbage butterfly and makes the cole plants tastier. Thyme *(Thymus)* is valued as a cabbageworm deterrent and helps accent the natural aroma of nearby plants. Rue *(Ruta graveolens)*, which is detested by rats, discourages Japanese beetles near roses and raspberries.

Tansy *(Tanacetum vulgare)* and pennyroyal *(Mentha pulegium)* help discourage ants. Tansy also deters flying insects, Japanese beetles, striped cucumber beetles, and squash bugs.

Basil mixes well with tomatoes both in salads and in the garden. Planted together, the basil will improve the tomatoes' flavor as well as growth (beebalm is thought to have the same effect); it also discourages flies and mosquitoes. However, basil is believed to hinder the growth of rue if planted next to it.

*Nasturtiums are believed to repel a wide range of harmful insects from plants, as well as to improve the growth and flavor of nearby crops.*

There are hundreds of other positive and negative combinations of herbs and other plants. For more detail, consult a book on the subject. Although the benefits of companion planting are not absolutely proven, many gardeners swear by it, and you may find it helpful in your garden.

# Pinching and Training

## Herbs That Benefit from Pinching

*Some herbs especially benefit from pinching or pruning to make them bushier and more productive. Basil, for example, produces much bushier plants if pinched and harvested regularly. When flowers start to form, pinch them off, too. Chervil flowers also displace leaf growth. Pinch off all but a few flowers, leaving one or two to set seed so that the plant will self-sow. Other herbs that thrive when pinched or harvested include coriander, costmary, horehound (in spring to keep tidy), lavender, lavender cotton, lemon balm, lemongrass, lemon verbena, marjoram, mint, oregano, sage, scented geraniums, sorrel (remove flowers), wormwood (in spring to keep from getting leggy), and yarrow (remove flowers to encourage new blooms).*

Most herbs flourish when they are cut back. Not only does this minor surgery improve the vigor of the plants, but it also encourages a bushier, more attractive form. Notice the response of plants, such as basil, that you harvest regularly for the kitchen. Whenever you remove a sprig, at least two new sprigs grow from the pair of leaves just below where you cut. Within a week or two, that new growth will be ready for harvest, doubling your potential take.

Even herbs that aren't edible, or that you use less frequently in the kitchen, benefit from a little pinching and pruning to maintain their strength and shapely form. Left to their own devices, many herbs grow long and weedy, but you can control that tendency with judicious care.

Many of the culinary herbs lose their flavor once they start to produce flowers. To delay the taste change, pinch off the developing flower heads on basil, chervil, costmary, lemon balm, lemon verbena, and oregano. Caraway, a biennial, will live another season if the flowers are removed. If you want some of your plants to self-seed, allow the flowers to develop on just a few of your plants, or let the flowers come on later in the season. Be sure to leave enough time for the seeds to develop and ripen properly.

In addition to pruning and pinching herbs to maintain their shape and increase their production, you can train certain herbs into topiary forms, especially the form called a standard, which is a plant trained to grow with a round, bushy globe on top of a tall, upright stem. The bay tree *(Laurus nobilis)* is a natural candidate for this kind of training since it naturally grows on a single stem. All you need to do is shape the top into a sphere, rather than letting it grow freely. This kind of treatment is especially appropriate in formal gardens. It also works well for bay trees

that will be brought indoors for winter, since the pruning keeps their size in check. In addition, try training upright-growing varieties of rosemary or scented geraniums as small standards.

To start a topiary, you will need a young plant with an unpinched leader, clippers, stakes (choose the thin-cane ones that are in scale with the small plant), ties, and patience. Each step takes only a few moments, but there is lots of waiting time in between as the plant grows.

Begin by tying the herb to the stake in three or four places along its stem. Keep the ties loose enough so as not to injure the stem, but tight enough to be effective. Keep the leaves along the trunk, but snip off any side shoots as they develop. By removing the side shoots, you'll encourage the plant to continue growing straight up, rather than bushing out. During the

**1** *Pinch off the flowers and top pair of leaves of young herbs such as basil to encourage bushier plants. Continue pinching back new growth for several weeks.*

# *Pinching and Training* CONTINUED

### Herbs for Topiary

*Many herbs are suitable for training into standards, spirals, and multiple levels. Some good candidates for topiaries are bay, curry plant, juniper, lavender, lavender cotton, lemon verbena, licorice plant, rosemary, sage, scented geraniums, and thyme.*

*To make stuffed sculptures planted in a frame, look for herbs and plants with vining or trailing habits such as chamomile, creeping thyme, feverfew, and sweet woodruff.*

active growing season, fertilize the plant with an all-purpose liquid fertilizer every fourth or fifth time you water. Feed less frequently as growth slows. Also turn the container every few days so that each side gets equal light and the plant grows straight up instead of reaching for the sun.

Depending on the growth rate of your herb and the final height you want it to reach, it can take four to six months or even longer for the plant to reach the appropriate height. As a guideline, a slow-growing, small-leaved plant looks attractive at 8 to 14 inches tall; let fast-growing plants with larger leaves grow as tall as 5 feet. Picture how you want the plant to look when it's finished, think about its setting, and grow it to have attractive proportions.

Once your topiary has reached the height you want, pinch off the tip of the leader. New sets of branches will develop at the top. Continue to prune and pinch these branches to develop a bushy head. Once you have a good set of foliage at the top, you can remove the leaflets along the plant's stem.

Another topiary shape that lends itself to herbs is the spiral. Follow the same directions as for a standard topiary, but prune the side shoots to create a spiraling effect. Use a string spiraled around the plant as a guide. Leave the spots long where the string lies along the plant, and prune the spaces in between close to the stem of the plant. If you lack the sculptural eye to prune this form with confidence, purchase a wire form and tie the young, supple plant to the frame.

*It's quite easy and fun to create topiaries out of herbs such as the santolina shown here. The finished masterpiece makes a classy contribution to a garden or patio design.*

**1** To make an herb topiary, first choose an appropriate-size pot for your mature topiary, and fill it with good potting soil.

**2** Insert the topiary frame. In addition to the globe form shown here, you can purchase spirals, hearts, and other fanciful shapes.

**3** Choose a young, flexible plant that has a growth habit that lends itself to your design. This rosemary plant has several branches.

**4** Plant the herb in your pot, and fill with additional soil as needed. Position the plant so that you can easily begin to train the shoots.

**5** Gently bend the side shoots to bring them onto the frame. Tie the shoots firmly, but not so tightly that the stems are damaged.

**6** Continue to train the plant as it grows, finally trimming it to maintain the desired form. Here the rosemary will form a compact globe shape.

# Propagation

*Although herbs that lend themselves to dividing (such as this lemon balm) can be propagated at any time of year, they adjust best if the divisions are taken in spring or fall.*

While most herbs can be readily grown from seed, they are also well suited to three other methods of propagation: division, cuttings, and layering. These methods are useful if you want to be sure you're getting an exact duplicate of a favorite variety.

### ▼ Division

Many herbs can be easily propagated by division. Some, such as chives, lemongrass, and oregano, grow in ever-expanding clumps. Others, including beebalm and mint, send out a broad network of roots that generate subsidiary shoots, which can be cut off as new plants.

The best time of year to divide plants is early spring, when they are just beginning their fresh burst of growth, or in fall in some places. In the north, where winter comes early, autumn is not a safe time to divide because the separated plants can't reestablish an adequate root system before the first freeze. In milder southern climates or in parts of the country where the first freeze comes fairly late in the season, autumn is a good time of year to multiply herbs by dividing them.

You can get away with dividing most plants even in the height of summer if you follow a few precautions. If possible, choose a cloudy day to make your summertime herb divisions. Otherwise, work in the evening, when the hot sun isn't stressing the plant. Give the plant a slow, deep watering about an hour before you plan to dig. Keep as much earth as

**1** Dig up the entire plant you want to divide, or use a sharp spade to cut through and remove the portion of the plant you want to propagate.

**2** Gently pull apart the plant into its individual sections, making sure each piece has both stems and roots. This sage can be pulled apart quite easily.

**3** Plant the divisions in a pot if they need careful nurturing, or replant them in the garden. Water them well until they are established.

**4** A small herb division will grow to a full-sized plant in just one growing season. After a few years, it can be divided again, and you'll get even more plants.

# *Propagation* CONTINUED

*If you cannot replant your
divided herbs immediately,
dip the root balls in water
and wrap them in plastic. Set
the plants in a sheltered spot
out of the sun, and plant
them as soon as possible.*

possible around the roots, and replant the division
immediately. If you are giving away the divided plant,
wrap the soil-covered roots in wet newspaper and
then in plastic. Give the new plant some protection
from the sun for the first few days, and water it frequently. It's possible the division will die back consid-
erably, but as long as the roots stay alive, you should
get new growth in autumn as the weather cools, as
well as the following spring.

In general, when dividing herbs, you can dig up the
entire plant and then cut or tear it into smaller pieces,
or simply insert a spade firmly into the middle of the
plant and through the roots and then remove one of
the split portions. Either way, plant the new divisions
immediately and water well. Replace the soil around
the exposed roots of the parent plant.

It is remarkable how many new plants can be sired
from one small clump. For example, chives can be
divided into portions as small as one blade with a bit
of root. Planted in spring, these small pieces will grow
into clumps several inches in diameter by the following year. Division is an excellent way to get enough
plants to edge a long bed.

With herbs such as chives, mint, and beebalm, it's
easy to see where the new plants are and how to separate them. On the other hand, lavender and lavender
cotton are a bit trickier. You have to be quite ruthless
about cutting through woody material to divide the
clump.

Garlic is usually propagated by dividing the bulbs
into individual cloves and planting them in the fall or
early spring. Soil rich in organic matter will grow the
biggest and best garlic bulbs.

**1** *Unearth an overgrown clump of garlic chives,
or cut through the middle of the clump with
force to take part of it.*

**5** *Split the clump in half, and then if necessary,
break or cut each half into quarters. A small division will multiply quickly.*

**2** A large clump of plants can be quite heavy. You may want to transport it in a wheelbarrow to a more convenient work area.

**3** To make a large clump of plants easier to see and handle, wash away the soil from the roots with a forceful spray of water.

**4** Use a trowel or shovel to cut through the roots. Aim between stems, but don't worry about damaging some of the plant.

**6** Once your clumps are small enough to handle more easily, tear them apart, separating them down to small clusters or even single stems.

**7** If you want to grow garlic chives indoors for winter, or prefer them in pots, replant a few divisions into good potting soil. Water well.

**8** Each of the single stem divisions from the large clump will grow into a sizable clump of its own within a year once planted in the garden.

# *Propagation* CONTINUED

**Herbs to Grow from Cuttings**

*These herbs reproduce readily from cuttings: beebalm, borage, catnip, horseradish (root cuttings), hyssop, lavender, lavender cotton, lemon balm, lemon verbena, marjoram, oregano, rosemary, sage, scented geraniums, sweet woodruff, tarragon, thyme, winter savory, and wormwood.*

*You can produce many lavender plants for a dramatic display by rooting cuttings taken from one plant.*

## ▼ Cuttings

Many herbs can be increased by taking cuttings. The three most common kinds of cuttings taken for herbs are softwood stem cuttings, semiripe or semihardwood heel cuttings, and basal stem cuttings. Softwood stem cuttings are taken in spring just as the tender new growth is beginning to mature. Semiripe heel cuttings are side shoots that have been pulled away from the main stem with a small heel of bark from the stem still attached. Take them in late summer or autumn before the stems become too woody. Basal stem cuttings should be taken in early spring, when the perennial herb first starts to sprout. Cut newly growing shoots from the bottom of the plant near the roots, including a small piece of basal wood, which is the brown, tough part of the stem.

Most herbs that can be propagated from cuttings root well from softwood taken in spring. A few exceptions that do better with semiripe heel cuttings taken later in the season include rosemary, wormwood (which also will root from softwood), bay, rue, sage, lavender cotton, and thyme. Feverfew roots best from basal stem cuttings.

A few hours before you plan to take softwood cuttings, water the plant thoroughly. Choose healthy sprouts that are freshly grown, and cut lengths 3 to 4

**1** Take semihardwood lavender cuttings in late summer or early fall. Use sharp clippers to cut 4- to 5-inch pieces from the tips of stems. Cut at an angle to allow for more surface area.

**2** Remove any forming seeds from the tip of the plant, and strip the leaves off the bottom half of each stem. If you like, dip each stem into a rooting hormone powder.

**3** Plant each cutting about 1 inch deep. A mixture of half vermiculite and half perlite is excellent for rooting because there is less chance of plant rot.

**4** The cuttings must be kept moist at all times. They also need warm temperatures, between 70° and 80°F. Here the cuttings are kept in a cold frame for better protection.

**5** You will know when your cuttings have rooted when you see new growth, or when you tug gently on the cutting and feel resistance. This means that the roots are becoming established.

**6** The following spring, when the cuttings have established healthy root systems and the weather has warmed, transplant the new plants into the garden.

# *Propagation* CONTINUED

**Herbs to Layer**

*Good candidates for propagation by layering include catnip, lavender, lavender cotton, rosemary (air layer), sage, thyme, and winter savory.*

inches long. Use sharp shears or a razor blade to make a clean cut. Make the cut at an angle, or recut it so that there is more surface area from which roots can grow. Plants tend to root better just below a node, so cut the stem there. Remove the bottom leaves, and pinch off any flowers or buds.

Cuttings can be rooted in a variety of media, both organic and inorganic. The important considerations are that you use a sterile mixture to inhibit possible disease and fungus and that the mix has a loose texture so that the tender new roots can push through easily. Cuttings will also root in water. Prepare the cut plant in the same way as you would to root it in a soil mixture, and put the stem in a glass of water. Roots will begin to form in a few weeks, although the exact length of time varies with the type of plant. Don't get discouraged; unless the slip wilts and rots, it is still viable. Add more water periodically to make up for evaporation, and change the water if it grows cloudy.

If you are rooting your cutting in a pot, be sure the medium is moist, but not dripping wet. Keep it damp and humid either by putting the cutting in a plastic bag to create a greenhouse-like environment (although do allow some airflow or the cutting could rot), or water and mist the cutting frequently. Keep the starting plant out of direct sun.

Geraniums have a very high sap content, which bleeds out for some time after the stems are cut. Wait about an hour after cutting scented geraniums before you put them in water or rooting medium (a vermiculite and perlite mix works well for them). This waiting time will allow the wound to seal, minimizing the possibility of the stem rotting.

When you notice new growth on the plant, you can be assured that roots have started to grow. You can

also check for roots by giving the plant a very gentle tug. If you feel resistance, the roots are growing.

Once the plant has a good root system, you can transfer it to a 6-inch or larger pot with potting soil, or put it directly into the garden. Follow with the hardening-off procedure described on page 67 to acclimate the new plant to the harsher outdoor environment.

## ▼ Layering

Many herbs will produce roots along a stem spontaneously if the branch lies undisturbed on moist soil. You can enhance this natural tendency by creating the conditions required for it to happen. The process is called layering. The best time of year to start a new plant by layering is in the spring or fall.

Choose a flexible branch or stem that will reach to the ground, and remove any foliage from the section you plan to root. Cut or scrape away the tough outer portion on the underside of the stem where it will touch the soil. Dust the wound with a rooting powder, and bury the treated section of branch, leaving about 6 inches of the tip end unburied. You may want to stake the end so that it can grow upright, rather than at an angle. If the plant you want to layer doesn't have stems that can easily touch the ground, place a pot filled with damp soil underneath a suitable stem. Be sure you keep the potted soil moist.

# Winter Preparation

*Rather than potting tender perennial herbs each fall to bring indoors for winter, grow them in pots all year. Keep the pots outside during the warm season, and then move them to a sheltered place, such as a porch, for a few weeks before bringing them inside. If you want them to look as if they were actually planted in the garden, bury the pots up to the rim. Burying will also help them stay more moist, so that you don't need to water as often.*

$A$t the end of the herb-growing year you'll want to prepare your garden beds for winter. In warm climates the job primarily entails removing spent annual herbs and tidying the garden. Rake away any debris that may have collected, and pull weeds. Mulch the beds to help keep down weeds during the rainy season and to give them a finished look. You can continue to harvest the perennial herbs throughout the winter, although be wary of taking too much and weakening the plants. They will be slightly less flavorful than they are in the hot summer. If you live where the soil freezes in winter, mulch after the ground has frozen solid.

In parts of the country where winters get cold, the herb garden requires more preparation. Trim back hardy perennial herbs by half of their new growth. If you want to bring tender perennials, such as rose-mary, pineapple-scented sage *(Salvia elegans)*, and lemon verbena *(Aloysia triphylla)* indoors for winter harvesting, cut back the plants to a manageable size and put them into pots in early autumn, then leave them outside in a protected spot until the really cold weather. These steps, which help the plants' transition to the new environment, are also appropriate for hardy perennials that you'd like to have inside. Another technique to prepare plants for the indoor habitat is to prune their roots and wait a few weeks for new feeder roots to grow. Then lift the plants out of the ground and pot them. Keep them in a sheltered spot for at least a few days before taking them inside.

The air indoors generally is much drier than what the plants are accustomed to outside. Rosemary is particularly sensitive and will lose all its leaves if you do not keep the air around it humid. Mist it regularly.

**1** *Mulch hardy perennials and biennials after the ground has frozen to protect roots from cold and prevent heaving caused by repeated freezes and thaws.*

**2** *In late autumn, before the winter cold settles in for the season, cut back hardy perennial herbs, such as this lemon balm, by half of their new growth.*

# *Winter Preparation* CONTINUED

Another method of enhancing the humidity around a plant is to set the pot on pebbles in a water-filled dish or tray. The evaporating water from the dish improves the humidity immediately around the plant to keep it moist.

Since most herbs require at least six hours of direct sun a day, you need to place your indoor herbs in a sunny window, preferably facing south. If you don't have enough natural light in your home, put the plants under artificial light. Fluorescent lights are fine for plants. Use a rig with either two or four tubes. You can either buy tubes that are color balanced to approximate sunlight or use a combination of cool white and warm white tubes. Set the lights 5 to 6 inches above the plants, and adjust them as the plants grow. To approximate six hours of sunlight, you need to keep the lights on for 14 to 16 hours a day.

Once the ground freezes for the first time, the hardy perennials that have been left outdoors should be mulched. This layer of mulch protects the roots from extreme cold, at the same time keeping the ground frozen so that it doesn't heave due to alternate periods of freezing and thawing. There are many organic materials that are excellent for mulching, including dry grass clippings, straw and hay, leaves, shredded newspaper, and bark. If you mulch annually, you will see a vast improvement in the quality of your soil over the years as the organic material breaks down and is mixed into the existing soil by worms. The mulch should be several inches thick.

Much of the winter information above doesn't apply to the mildest climates where frost is rare and short-lived. In fact, in tropical and subtropical regions, you can grow most annual as well as perennial herbs throughout the year. See the section on temperature considerations on pages 60–61 for more information on growing herbs year-round in warm climates.

**Bringing Chives Indoors**

*Chives are perennials that die to the ground in cold winter climates, returning in spring. However, if you bring them into the warmth, they will remain green and grow all winter.*

*Prepare a 5-inch pot with a drainage hole in the bottom. Put a piece of screen or pot shard over the hole so that dirt doesn't wash out, and partially fill the pot with good potting soil. Dig up a clump (or part of a large clump) of chives, and plant it in the pot, adding extra soil as needed. Then cut back the chives to allow the roots to establish themselves. Leave the pots outdoors long enough to expose them to four to six weeks of freezing temperatures. Then bring the chives indoors to a sunny windowsill.*

**1** To continue harvesting your herbs into winter, choose a healthy-looking specimen from the garden and dig it up with a trowel or spade.

**2** Transfer the plant to a pot large enough to house the roots comfortably. Make sure there is adequate drainage in the pot.

**3** Keep your newly potted herbs in a protected spot, such as a porch or under eaves, for a week or more before moving them indoors.

**4** Place your indoor herbs in a bright, sunny window or under lights. You can harvest the herbs through much of the winter.

EARTH · WISE
TIP

*Not all lavender is winter hardy. If you live in a very cold climate, be sure you grow a type that can survive the winter. In addition to extremely cold temperatures, heavy, wet soil will kill lavender (as well as tarragon, sage, and thyme). Don't put these plants in low-lying areas where water may collect, and make sure they are growing in well-drained soil. If winter rain and snow are problems, cover the plants with a waterproof box to keep off excess moisture.*

# Herbs

### Spring

### Summer

**COOL CLIMATES**

- About six weeks before the last frost in your area, start herb seeds indoors to get a head start on the outdoor growing season.

- Prepare the garden beds for planting. Although herbs can survive in poor soil, they do better in good-quality soil that drains well. If you have heavy clay soil, amend it with sand, vermiculite, perlite, and lots of organic matter to make it lighter and improve drainage.

- Begin weeding early in the season, before the weeds' roots get too developed and before they set seed.

- Once the weather has warmed, set out new plants you have purchased this year. This is also the time to divide large plants and take cuttings to increase your supply of a favorite herb.

- As you harvest herb leaves, pinch back the plants to shape them and promote bushier growth.

- As the number of leaves available for harvest increases, take some to dry for winter use. Either tie bundles together and hang them upside down in a warm, well-ventilated spot out of direct sun, or spread leaves out on screens stapled onto frames that are stacked to allow airflow. If you are drying only a few leaves, simply clean them and leave them loose on a paper towel.

- Make herbal vinegars. Modify the proportions depending on how strong a flavor you want, but the basic ratio is one cup of fresh herb per quart of vinegar (white, cider, or red wine vinegar is fine). Cover the herb with vinegar in a glass container, seal, and store for two to four weeks until the vinegar is imbued with the herbal flavor.

**WARM CLIMATES**

- Start seeds of annual herbs indoors to get a head start on the growing season.

- Prepare the soil for new plantings. Although herbs can survive in poor soil, they do better in good-quality soil that drains well. If you have heavy clay soil, add vermiculite, sand, perlite, and lots of organic matter to loosen the soil and improve drainage.

- Sow seeds directly in the ground for herbs that grow better if they aren't transplanted (see the sidebar on page 70).

- Begin weeding early in the season, before the weeds' roots get too developed and before they set seed.

- If you see signs of whiteflies or mealybugs (the latter deposit a white, fluffy substance on the leaves), remove them with a strong spray of water from a hose or with damp paper towels. If you have a major infestation, spray with an insecticidal soap.

- Water your garden when necessary. A slow, deep watering is more effective than frequent sprinkles. Slow irrigation allows water to get down to the roots, encouraging them to grow deeper, making the plant more drought tolerant.

- Remove developing flower heads from plants such as basil, chervil, costmary, lemon balm, lemon verbena, oregano, rosemary, and tarragon. The leaves are more flavorful if the flowers aren't allowed to develop. Caraway, a biennial, will live an extra season if its flowers are removed.

- Start drying herbs for cooking, indoor arrangements, or potpourris. Follow the drying instructions on pages 100–103.

## Fall

- Prepare tender perennials to be moved indoors by pruning their roots early in the season. Once new feeder roots have grown, lift them out of the ground, pot them, and put them in a protected spot, such as a porch or under the eaves. Before the first frost, move them indoors to a bright, sunny window or put them under lights.

- Sow seeds of cool-season herbs, such as chervil, coriander, and parsley. If your winters are extremely cold, grow these herbs in a cold frame or on a sunny windowsill.

- To grow oregano, tarragon, and mint indoors for continual winter harvesting, divide mature plants and pot them now. Cut back the plants severely, water well, and bring them indoors, where they will continue to grow. To get chives to thrive indoors, give them at least a few weeks of dormancy in a cool area after potting them up.

- Clean up the garden, removing dead plants, weeds, leaves, and other debris. Compost any organic material that isn't diseased.

- Sow seeds of cool-season herbs, such as chervil, coriander, and parsley, for your second winter crop.

- Clean up the garden, removing dead plants, weeds, leaves, and other debris. Compost any organic waste that hasn't been infested with pests or disease. A fall cleaning will help prevent diseases and pests next year.

- Continue to use or freeze herbs. For example, dig up large horseradish roots, peel them, and grind them in a food processor. Puree the ground root with a little water and vinegar. If you plan to use it right away, mix a portion with sour cream and sugar. Freeze the rest of the puree in ice cube trays for future use.

## Winter

- Mulch your herb plants after the ground begins to freeze.

- About six weeks before the warm spring weather arrives, take cuttings from the tender perennial herbs you have overwintered indoors. They will take three to six weeks to root and be ready to plant outside in spring.

- Read catalogues and books about herbs to learn about new plant varieties you might like to try and to get new ideas for ways to use herbs in your home and garden.

- Make potpourris, sachets, and wreaths with your dried herbs. Enjoy a hot cup of herbal tea.

- Soak in an herbal bath. Try bay, lemon balm, lemongrass, mint, or thyme. Experiment with mixtures. Place one cup of dried herb leaves into a cheesecloth bag or nylon stocking, cover with water, and bring to a boil. Steep for 15 minutes, then add the water to your bath.

- Read catalogues and books about herbs to learn about new plant varieties you might like to try and to get new ideas for ways to use herbs in your home and garden.

- Make potpourris, sachets, and wreaths with your dried herbs. Enjoy a hot cup of herbal tea made with dried herbs from your garden.

- Soak in an herbal bath. Try bay, lemon balm, lemongrass, mint, or thyme. Experiment with different blends. Place one cup of dried herb leaves into a cheesecloth bag or nylon stocking. Cover with water in a saucepan, and bring to a boil. Steep for 15 minutes, then add the water to your bath.

*This table offers a basic outline of garden care by season. The tasks for each season differ for warm and cool climates: warm climates correspond to USDA plant hardiness zones 8 through 11, and cool climates to zones 2 through 7. Obviously, there are substantial climate differences within these broad regions. To understand the specific growing conditions in your area, consult the zone map on page 127. Also be sure to study local factors affecting the microclimate of your garden, such as elevation and proximity of water.*

# CHAPTER 4

# Harvesting and Using Herbs

*h*erbs are a joy to grow in the garden, and they have a wealth of applications in your home. In addition to their culinary uses, their medicinal properties are legendary. • Today, as in the past, herbs are a popular ingredient in cosmetic products, including bath oils and shampoos. Many herbs are valued for their colors, which make vibrant natural dyes. The pungent scents of many herbs can be captured for potpourris and sachets, and they can be preserved for future use by drying or freezing. • Herbs can also be wonderful additions to both dried- and fresh-flower arrangements, wreaths, and other home-decorating and craft projects.

# Harvesting Herbs

The best time to harvest herbs is mid-morning, when the sun has dried the dew off the leaves, but before the summer heat has dissipated the plants' oils. However, many cooks prefer to step outside and snip the herbs just as they need them. If you harvest the herbs in mid-morning but don't need to use them until later in the day, put the stems in a glass of water and keep them out of direct sun.

Herbs that are grown for their roots, such as garlic, shallots, and orris, should be harvested in fall, after the leaves start to yellow and die down.

Annual herbs, which by nature grow quickly, benefit from frequent harvesting. The more you pick, the more the plant will produce, and as a result, you'll get a nice, bushy plant form. Other culinary herbs that benefit from frequent harvesting throughout the growing season include chives, mint, marjoram, rosemary, parsley, sage, and thyme.

Many herb flowers are edible and make attractive additions to salads, desserts, and other dishes. Harvest the flowers of borage, violets, chives, garlic, roses, hyssop, pot marigolds, rosemary, fennel, and beebalm when they are in fresh bloom. Pick herb flowers early in the day, as you would blooms for cutting, and keep them in water until you are ready to use them. Be sure that plants whose flowers you plan to eat have not been treated with any poisons, including systemic fertilizers.

Harvest seeds of herbs when they are ripe. To avoid losing the ripe seeds when you shake them loose from the plant, tie a paper bag around the ripening seed heads to catch any seeds that fall.

**1** *Pick or cut the outer leaves of parsley, but don't disturb the inner growing point. The leaves are less flavorful once flowers form.*

**4** *Harvest lavender for sachets and potpourris in late morning, when the plants are drier. Cut flowers before they open fully.*

**2** *Harvest dill just before the seeds are completely ripe to prevent self-sowing. Or you can wait and harvest the fully-ripened seeds from the dill.*

**3** *Dig up your garlic in late summer when the tops begin to die down. For the biggest bulbs next summer, choose some of the cloves to plant immediately.*

**E A R T H • W I S E**
**T I P**

*Resist heavy harvesting from first-year perennial herbs. Harvesting stimulates new leaf growth, and in the first year it is better for the plant's energy to go toward establishing a good root system.*

**5** *It's most efficient to harvest basil by pinching back the plants. At the same time you will shape them and promote bushier growth.*

# Drying Herbs

Whether you plan to use your dried herbs in flower arrangements, for cooking, or for potpourris, your goal is to dry them as quickly as possible to avoid shrinking and fading. The best drying technique depends on the herb's intended use.

For arrangements, pick fairly long stems, then strip off all the lower leaves. Gather the plants into small, loose bunches so that the air can circulate freely, and fasten them with rubber bands. (The rubber bands constrict as the stems dry and shrink. Stems tend to fall out of bundles tied with string.) Hang the herb bunches upside down in a hot, dry, well-ventilated area, such as an attic or garage. You also can hang herbs in a spare room that has a fan to keep the air moving. Keep drying plants out of direct sun, which will fade their color and dissipate their oils. Yarrow, tansy, rose hips, red peppers, and plants with pretty foliage are well suited to air drying for arrangements.

Dry large amounts of culinary herbs on drying screens that are stacked on legs to allow plenty of air circulation. To make your own drying screen, stretch and staple a window screen onto a wooden frame, and attach 4-inch-long blocks to the four corners for legs. For large-leaved herbs, such as basil, strip off the individual leaves and scatter them on the screen in a single layer. Chop chives and lemongrass before you dry them. Dry whole sprigs of small-leaved plants, such as thyme and rosemary, and strip off the leaves when they are ready for storage.

If you are preserving just a handful of herbs, simply wash them, pat them dry, and lay them flat on a cloth or paper towel. In a few days, they will be dry enough to store in labeled glass jars. Keep empty spice jars to store your homegrown and dried herbs. If you notice moisture forming inside the sealed jar, take the herbs out and dry them a few more days.

**1** *A portable laundry rack is excellent for drying herbs. Hang the herbs upside down in small bunches. Keep in a warm, dry room out of direct light.*

Herbs for potpourris can be dried in an oven, microwave, dehydrator, or desiccant such as silica gel, borax, or a mixture of borax and cornmeal. Each method has its advantages and disadvantages.

Oven drying is useful because it doesn't take a lot of effort. For electric ovens, set the temperature at 100°F (leave the oven door ajar if your thermostat can't be set that low), and dry herbs in a single layer on a baking sheet. Check periodically, and remove them when they are thoroughly dry. Preheat a gas oven to 180°F, turn it off, and set your herbs inside on a baking sheet. Leave them for several days; the oven will retain the heat from the pilot light. Don't forget to take the herbs out before you preheat the oven for baking or roasting. Herb flowers retain their color when oven-dried, but they do tend to shrink.

**2** *Clip or tie bundles of herbs onto coat hangers, then hang them in a warm closet. Be sure to allow enough space between the herbs for air to circulate.*

**3** *Another method of drying herbs is to loosely pack herbs into manila envelopes or brown paper bags. Hang the packages on the wall or set in the corner to dry.*

Microwave drying shrinks flowers less than a conventional oven and works well in an emergency, when you need dried herbs quickly. Place your herbs in a single layer between two white paper towels. Run the microwave at medium power for one minute. Check the plant for dryness, and then heat it for another minute at medium power. Continue heating and checking until the material is dry. Keep notes of the drying time of each plant for future reference.

Dehydrating machines are very effective for drying culinary herbs because they work quickly, retaining the flavorful oils in the leaves and not allowing time for dust to accumulate. However, these heated boxes shrink flowers and are not as useful if you want a potpourri that looks pretty.

*Oregano, basil, sage, celeriac, dill, and mint are just some of the many herbs you can dry for winter cooking. These versatile herbs can also be enjoyed in wreaths and other homemade creations.*

# *Drying Herbs* CONTINUED

Powdered desiccants are an excellent way to dry flowers so that they retain their colors and shapes. Pour about an inch of the desiccant into an airtight box. Set the flower face down on the powder, arranging the petals carefully with a toothpick. Sift in additional desiccant, adjusting the petals as necessary until the flower is covered. You can dry several layers of flowers in one container, but be careful not to squash them. Cover the container tightly so that it is properly sealed, and wait.

Silica gel takes two to three days to dry most plant materials. Check the flowers after two days because the gel will cause them to fade once they are dry. Also, flowers dried in silica will reabsorb water from the air. This drying method is best for arrangements you plan to keep in a controlled atmosphere, such as under glass.

Borax, a widely-used laundry additive, is 75 percent less expensive than silica gel and doesn't fade the flowers as much. Borax takes three to five days to dry herbs, depending on how much moisture is in the plant. Another excellent desiccant is one part borax mixed with three to four parts cornmeal. This combination takes a day or two longer to dry the plants, but the flowers will keep their color better. Check the flowers in three to four days by gently brushing aside the powder until you reveal the herbs.

These desiccant powders can be reused five or six times. Sift the medium to remove any plant bits that may have broken loose. Silica gel has blue crystals that turn pink when the material is saturated with water. The color change is your indication that you have exhausted the usefulness of that batch.

Seeds are dried in the same way as foliage; however, they need to be separated from their casings, called chaff. Generally it's easier to do this when the entire head has dried. Rub the seeds between your hands to loosen the chaff, put everything in a shallow dish, and blow gently across the seeds. The light chaff will blow away, leaving the heavier seeds. Gently shake the dish to raise additional chaff to the top, and blow again.

Roots are generally air-dried. Orris, which is superb for fixing the aroma of a potpourri, should be peeled and chopped into coarse pieces before laying it out in a single layer to dry. Once it is thoroughly dry, chop it finely in the food processor. Alternatively, slice it very thin with a potato slicer to make paper-thin chips that look lovely in a potpourri.

# Freezing Herbs

Many herbs that don't dry well, including basil, dill, parsley, chervil, chives, and fennel, are excellent to freeze. Freezing herbs is very easy. In most cases simply wash the herbs and pat them dry, spread them in a single layer on a pan, and put them in the freezer. Chop chives and lemongrass before you freeze them. Because herbs are thin, they will freeze within minutes. Then put them into labeled, sealed containers and keep them in the freezer. Zip-lock freezer bags are handy for freezing herbs (push out all the air before you seal them), as are airtight plastic containers. In most cases, you don't need to bother to thaw these herbs before you use them.

Another tasty way to freeze herbs is to make a paste by mixing ⅓ cup of oil with 2 cups of herbs in a blender until smooth. The paste freezes beautifully in sealed jars or in ice cube trays that are thoroughly wrapped to make them airtight. The paste will also keep for about a week in the refrigerator. In winter, retrieve a frozen paste to give a fresh taste to your dishes. Herbs that are good candidates for grinding into pastes include basil, chervil, cilantro, coriander, dill, fennel, marjoram, mint, parsley, rosemary, sage, savory, and tarragon.

Herbs can also be frozen to make decorative ice cubes for party drinks. Freeze strawberries and their leaves, mint sprigs, and woodruff sprigs into an ice ring or block. Boil the water first to make it clear. Once it has cooled, fill the bottom of the mold with the boiled water and freeze. Arrange the herbs you plan to freeze, then continue adding water until the mold is filled.

**Herbs That Freeze Well**
*Some herbs will keep their flavor when frozen. Simply clean the leaves, dry them, and put them in sealed plastic bags (remove all the air before sealing) or another airtight container. Try these herbs: basil, borage, chives, dill (better frozen than dried), lemongrass, mint, oregano, sage, savory (both winter and summer), sorrel (better than dried), sweet woodruff, tarragon, and thyme.*

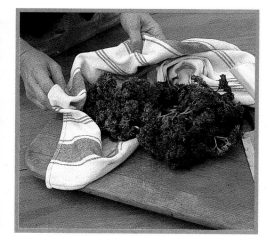

**1** *To freeze parsley, first rinse and dry the leaves.*

**2** *Chop the parsley leaves into fine pieces.*

**3** *Place in freezer bags, label, and seal well.*

# Cooking with Herbs

*You can flavor bottles of oil or vinegar by inserting some fresh herbs. Allow the infusions to steep for two to four weeks, depending on how strong you like the flavor.*

There is a long list of herbs valuable as seasonings. Many, such as coriander and caraway, are associated with particular national cuisines. There are classic French herb blends, including one known as *fines herbes*, which is comprised of equal parts parsley, tarragon, chives, and chervil, and *bouquet garni*, a blend of parsley, thyme, and bay leaf used for flavoring soups, stews, sauces, braised meat, and vegetables. Often, herbs for bouquet garni are tied into a cheesecloth, so the entire bundle is easy to remove before serving the dish.

Herbs can also be combined with oils and vinegar. Leave a few cloves of peeled garlic in olive oil to give it extra zest for salads, or add a cup of your favorite fresh herb to a quart of vinegar and allow it to steep for two to four weeks (the length of time you wait depends on how strong you like the flavor).

Herbal butters are made by creaming chopped herbs into softened butter. Make herbal butter balls or cubes, pack the butter into a small crock, or make fanciful shapes by pressing it into chocolate molds (put them into the freezer to make them firm, then remove from the mold). You can freeze herbal butters for several months.

When cooking with herbs, remember that dried herbs have a more concentrated flavor than fresh ones. If you are using fresh herbs for a recipe that calls for dry, increase the amount by about three times. Thawed frozen herbs can be used in the same proportion as fresh, but taste as you go and experiment to develop your own special recipes.

# *Herbal Healing*

*I*n the days before antibiotics, herbal remedies were used to treat many ailments. Herbal teas in the seventeenth century were promulgated as cure-alls, and according to a popular concept called the Doctrine of Signatures, plants were chosen as cures for the body organ they resembled.

In the past, physicians and herbalists struggled to understand and harness the healing drugs available in nature. Today, herbs, or their synthesized active ingredients, continue to be vital tools in modern medicine. For example, foxglove is still used to produce digitalis for heart disease, and morphine extracted from poppies is important for pain relief. Mint is a natural disinfectant. Commercially it is used in face masks, facial steams, toothpaste, and herbal baths.

Herbal teas have long been enjoyed not only for their refreshing, delicious taste, but also for their medicinal benefits. Raspberry tea is reputed to tone the uterus in anticipation of giving birth; rosemary tea is supposed to ease rheumatic pain and indigestion, as well as fatigue. Drink mint tea to alleviate indigestion and lavender tea to relieve tension headaches.

One of the best ways to use herbs' healing qualities is in the bath. Try rosemary when you are particularly tired, mint to soothe nervous exhaustion, and thyme to reduce swelling and sprains. Use either fresh or dried herbs, but tie them in cheesecloth so that they don't clog the drain.

There are many other forms in which herbs can be used for healing purposes. They can be made into poultices, compresses, tinctures, decoctions, syrups, ointments, creams, and oils, bringing comfort to both mind and body.

*Throw a handful of fresh mint leaves into a tea pot, cover with boiling water, and allow to steep for several minutes. You'll discover the joys of a tangy mint tea.*

# Using Herbs in the Home

**Potpourri**

*In French, pot pourri means, literally, "rotten pot." Today, however, "potpourri" has come to mean quite the opposite of rotten. A wonderfully fragrant mixture of herbs and spices bound with essential oils and fixatives, potpourri is used to give a room a subtle, gentle scent. Here's a basic potpourri recipe that can be varied to include your favorite plants and fragrances:*

*Mix 3 tablespoons of powdered orrisroot with 1 teaspoon of essential oil, such as rose oil. Blend and store, covered, for a few days, shaking occasionally. This allows the orrisroot to absorb the moisture of the oil.*

*Mix in 1 quart of dried flowers and herbs. Add 2 to 3 tablespoons of spices. Mix well and store, covered, in a container for four to six weeks, stirring occasionally.*

*Pack the potpourri in jars or baskets to keep, to give as gifts, or to crush and use in sachets.*

There is more you can do with herbs than cook and heal with them. They are the prime ingredients of fragrant potpourris and sachets. You can also use herbs and other plants to make natural dyes for both clothes and Easter eggs.

A potpourri is a delightfully scented blend that not only smells fragrant but also looks pretty in a decorative bowl. In it dried herbal ingredients are combined with oils, spices, and fixatives (dried ground or chopped orrisroot is an effective fixative, enhancing and preserving the aroma of any mix). You can make a one-scent potpourri with flowers such as lavender or rose petals, or combine different dried herbs such as lemon verbena and lemon balm to create a fruity blend. Add cloves and cinnamon for a spicy edge. Make a "remembrance" potpourri by using the flowers from a wedding bouquet or other special occasion.

Lady's-mantle, bay, pot marigold, onion, catnip, parsley, rue, and tansy are just a few of the herbs from which colors can be extracted for dye, either from their flowers, foliage, or roots. Have fun experimenting with the different effects, intensities, and colors, and explore how the dyes respond to different fabrics and surfaces. You'll be sharing in a process of trial and error that dates back to early civilization.

For special gifts, try making tussie-mussies. These little bouquets or nosegays were originally carried by both men and women in medieval days so that they could bury their noses in the sweet-scented flowers and herbs when the odors of the streets became overwhelming. Just create a small but tight posy with lots of scented flowers and herbs, and tie the stems together. Then cut an "x" in the center of a stiff doily and insert the bouquet.

*Make a single-scent potpourri with just one flower or herb, or combine different complementary scents to create a medley.*

Make herbal wreaths with fresh herbs set into circular oasis wells for a tabletop display, or wire dried herbs to a wreath frame to make a long-lasting wreath to hang on a door or wall. The use of herbs in your home is limited only by your energy, inclination, and imagination.

**1** *For an herbal wreath, begin with a frame. You can work with a twig form (as shown here), a wire frame, or a florist foam cut to a ring.*

**2** *Gather the dried materials you want to use. Choose a variety of shapes and textures, such as round garlic cloves and broad, flat leaves.*

**3** *Wire all the dried material to the form. Generally the wreath looks better if you pack the foliage quite close together.*

**4** *Step back to inspect your work periodically, and add extra material where the wreath looks unfinished.*

**5** *To complete your wreath, add fruit or berries to give it a festive look. It will make an ideal tabletop centerpiece.*

**6** *Hang the wreath in a place where you can enjoy both its subtle scent and its attractive appearance.*

# Herbs for American Gardens

This section provides concise information on more than 90 herbs recommended for American gardens. Favorites like basil and oregano are covered, as well as less common herbs, such as clary sage and mint marigold. The table contains descriptions of the plants and the useful parts, growing conditions, directions for planting, and harvesting tips. Each entry includes a photograph of the herb.

### ▼ About Plant Names

Plants appear in alphabetical order by the common name, shown in bold type. On the next line are other widely used common names. When there is more than one entry for a type of herb, such as Corsican mint and peppermint, the entries are listed under the type—in this case, "mint." Shown in italics is the complete botanical name: genus, species, and where applicable, the variety or cultivar.

When several species in a genus are similar in appearance and cultural needs, such as Greek oregano and golden oregano, they are listed together in a single entry in the chart. Most entries, however, describe one particular plant or type of plant.

The second column of the table provides a brief description of the plant and the useful portion. Look here for information on the plant's uses in the garden as well as in the home.

### ▼ Time of Bloom

Some herbs have beautiful flowers that add lively ornamental value to the garden. Many of these flowers, such as lavender, can also be dried. In this column, bloom time is given by season. Remember that the time of bloom for each herb will vary somewhat from one region of the country to another according to climate, weather, and growing conditions.

### ▼ Height and Spread

This column of the table lists the average mature height and spread of the plant. Since herbs are often used for ornamental purposes in the garden, it is important to know whether the plant is tall, shrubby, or a ground cover.

### ▼ Uses

In the next column you will find descriptions of the most common uses for the herb, such as culinary applications, potpourris and other crafts, or simple healing possibilities.

### ▼ Hardiness Zones

For perennial herbs, hardiness zones are given. These zones correspond to the newest version of the USDA Plant Hardiness Zone Map, shown on page 127.

Annual herbs are listed as hardy, half-hardy, or tender. Hardy plants can tolerate quite a bit of frost and can be planted outdoors in early spring as soon as the soil can be worked. Half-hardy plants can tolerate some light frost but are damaged by prolonged exposure to cold. Plant them outside when the danger of heavy frost is past, although occasional light frosts may still occur.

Tender herbs cannot withstand any frost at all. Do not plant them in the garden until all danger of frost is past (a week or two after the average last frost date for your area) and the soil is warming.

### ▼ Growing Conditions

The last column of the chart summarizes the best growing conditions for the plant. Look here for information on sun, soil, and moisture needs. Sowing, transplanting, propagating, pruning, and harvesting tips also appear here.

| | | | Time of Bloom | Height & Spread | Uses | Hardiness Zones | Growing Conditions |
|---|---|---|---|---|---|---|---|
| | **ACONITE**<br>MONKSHOOD,<br>WOLFSBANE<br>*Aconitum napellus* | A perennial with spikes of helmet-shaped, dark blue-violet or white flowers on tall stems with decorative dark green, deeply lobed leaves. All parts of this plant are poisonous. | Mid-summer to mid-autumn | Height: 3–5'<br><br>Spread: 1–2' | In the past this toxic plant was used in liniments. Use only for ornamental purposes. | 3 to 8 | Full sun to partial shade. Deep, rich, moist, well-drained soil. A slow-growing perennial that performs best in a cool climate, aconite should be divided every several years. |
| | **ANGELICA**<br>*Angelica archangelica* | A bold, celery-like addition to the herb garden. Tall purple stems have large (1–2 ft.), 3-part leaves with clasping bases. Tiny light green or white flowers are arranged in 6- to 8-in., globular clusters. | Early summer | Height: 5–8'<br><br>Spread: 2–4' | Stems, roots, leaves, and seeds used as a sweetener, in herbal teas, in salads, or candied. Dried leaves produce a green dye. | 4 to 10 | Partial shade. Moist to wet, humus-rich soil. Treat this short-lived perennial as a biennial, sowing seeds $1/4$ in. deep in early spring. Aphids may be a problem. |
| | **ANISE**<br>*Pimpinella anisum* | An annual herb whose feathery, compound leaves and $1/8$-in., oval seeds are grown for their pungent licorice flavoring. Erect stems emerge from long taproots and bear tiny light yellow flowers in 3-in., flat-topped clusters. | Summer | Height: $1 1/2$–2'<br><br>Spread: $1 1/2$' | Seeds and leaves give licorice flavor to herbal teas, baked goods, fruits, confections, and liqueurs (anisette); also used to aid digestion. | Half-hardy annual | Full sun. Well-drained soil of average fertility. Sow seeds $1/4$ in. deep in mid-spring, spacing rows 2–3 ft. apart. Plants grow best in warm sun; shelter from strong winds. Harvest seeds by clipping entire seed heads as they mature. |
| | **ANISE HYSSOP**<br>BLUE GIANT HYSSOP<br>*Agastache foeniculum* | A perennial of the mint family whose leaves have a fragrance reminiscent of anise or fennel. The 3-in. leaves are medium green above and white below. The 4-in. spikes of tiny, tubular, lilac-blue flowers attract bees. | Late spring to late summer | Height: 2–3'<br><br>Spread: 1–$1 1/2$' | Leaves and flowers used in potpourris, sachets, and herbal teas. | 3 to 8 | Full sun to light shade. Rich, well-drained soil. Once established, anise hyssop spreads slowly by rhizomes and by self-sowing. |
| | **BASIL**<br>SWEET BASIL<br>◄ *Ocimum basilicum*<br>SPICY GLOBE BASIL<br>*O. basilicum* 'Spicy Globe' | An annual grown for its smooth, 2- to 4-in. leaves used to flavor a wide variety of dishes. There are many cultivars varying in leaf color, flavor, and size. 'Spicy Globe' forms 1-ft.-high mounds with tiny, intensely flavored leaves. | Mid-summer | Height: 1–2'<br><br>Spread: 6–12" | Leaves used to flavor salads, pasta, tomatoes, cheese, pesto, meat, and poultry. | Tender annual | Full sun. Humus-rich, moist, well-drained soil. Sow seeds $1/8$ in. deep after frost, or start indoors in early spring. Basil grows best in warm weather. Remove flower buds to keep plants bushy and vigorous. |

◄ Indicates species shown

# Herbs for American Gardens

| | | Time of Bloom | Height & Spread | Uses | Hardiness Zones | Growing Conditions |
|---|---|---|---|---|---|---|
| **BAY**<br>LAUREL<br>*Laurus nobilis* | An evergreen tree whose 1- to 3-in., glossy, lance-shaped leaves were woven into wreaths to crown victorious athletes and warriors in classical times. The aromatic dark green leaves turn light green as they dry. | Spring | Height: 5–10' (40' in wild)<br>Spread: 4–11' | Dried leaves used extensively in stews, soups, and sauces; also in herbal teas as a digestive aid. Ornamental small tree. | 8 to 11 | Full sun to partial shade. Moist, well-drained, humus-rich soil. Propagate this slow-growing plant from cuttings. Bay can be grown in a tub or container; bring it indoors in winter north of zone 8. Prune to restrain size if necessary. |
| **BEEBALM**<br>BERGAMOT<br>*Monarda didyma* | A perennial that attracts hummingbirds, bees, and butterflies with its bright clusters of red, 2-lipped flowers borne on slender, square stems. The pairs of lanced-shaped leaves smell citrusy. Cultivars come in several flower colors. | Early to late summer | Height: 2–3'<br>Spread: 6–12" | Leaves and flowers used in herbal teas, salads, beverages, and potpourris. Ornamental flowers. | 4 to 8 | Full sun to partial shade. Moist (or even wet), well-drained, humus-rich soil. Beebalm is prone to mildew when crowded. Divide plants periodically to maintain vigor and keep in check. Harvest leaves and flowers as needed. |
| **BETONY**<br>*Stachys officinalis*<br>LAMB'S-EARS<br>*S. byzantina* | A perennial member of the mint family with hairy stems and coarse, deep green leaves rich in tannin. Tubular, 2-lipped, purple flowers cluster in whorled spikes around the stem. S. byzantina has soft, velevety leaves. | Mid- to late summer | Height: 2–3'<br>Spread: 6–12" | Fresh or dried leaves used in herbal teas. Ornamental spikes of flowers. | 5 to 11 | Full sun to partial shade. Evenly moist, well-drained soil of average fertility. Betony forms tidy clumps; it does not spread like other mints. Harvest leaves as needed. |
| **BORAGE**<br>*Borago officinalis* | A bee-attracting annual grown since classical times for its clusters of clear blue-violet flowers. The 3/4-in. flowers look like 5-pointed stars with protruding stamens. The fuzzy, gray-green leaves have a cucumber-like fragrance. | Early summer to frost | Height: 1–2'<br>Spread: 1–1 1/2' | Mince young leaves for herbal teas, salads, and vegetables; use flowers as garnish and in salads. Ornamental flowers and foliage. | Hardy annual | Full sun to light shade; afternoon shade in zones 8–11. Sow seeds where desired at monthly intervals for continuous bloom. Deadhead withering flowers to prolong blooming. Borage self-sows but does not transplant well. |
| **BOXWOOD**<br>COMMON BOXWOOD<br>*Buxus sempervirens* | A slow-growing shrub with small evergreen leaves and slender green branches. The 3/4-in., deep green leaves have a pungent aroma. Boxwood is excellent for hedges or a dark green backdrop; it takes pruning well. | Spring | Height: 15–20'<br>Spread: 15–20' | Cut twigs used in wreaths. Ornamental foliage. Prune to make a low border hedge for herb gardens. | 6 to 10 | Full sun to light shade. Moist, well-drained soil. Plant boxwood where it will be protected from drying winds. Plants have shallow roots, so do not disturb the soil in the immediate vicinity. |

| | | | Time of Bloom | Height & Spread | Uses | Hardiness Zones | Growing Conditions |
|---|---|---|---|---|---|---|---|
| | **CALENDULA** POT MARIGOLD *Calendula officinalis* | *An old-fashioned annual whose cheery flowers are used as a culinary herb. The 2- to 4-in., marigold-like flowers range from cream to yellow to orange. The pale green leaves have a pungent aroma.* | *Late spring to early autumn* | Height: 1–2' Spread: 1–1½' | *Flowers add flavor and color to soups, stews, and poultry; also used in herbal baths and to produce a yellow dye.* | Hardy annual | *Full sun to light shade. Evenly moist, well-drained soil. Sow seeds ⅓ in. deep where desired in fall or early spring. Easy-to-grow calendula can be planted in a pot or a cutting garden. Remove faded blooms to prolong flowering.* |
| | **CARAWAY** *Carum carvi* | *A relative of the carrot with the flat-topped clusters of tiny white or pinkish flowers, clasping ferny leaves, and thick roots typical of its family. The seeds and leaves of this biennial are used as culinary herbs.* | *Late spring to early summer* | Height: 1–2' Spread: 6–12"￼ | *Seeds used to flavor soups, stews, rye bread, and cheese. Chopped leaves are used in vegetable and egg dishes.* | 3 to 11 | *Full sun. Moist, well-drained soil. Sow seeds ¼–½ in. deep in early spring. This biennial sometimes flowers the first year. Once established, it may self-sow. Harvest seed heads just as they turn brown. Aphids can be a problem.* |
| | **CATMINT** *Nepeta × faassenii* | *A perennial herb grown as much for its showy clusters of ½-in., blue or lavender flowers as for its aromatic, gray-green, 1¼-in. leaves. Catmint forms mounds with age. Like other members of the mint family, it has squarish stems.* | *Late spring to mid-summer* | Height: 2–3' Spread: 1–1½' | *Leaves used in cat treats and herbal teas.* | 3 to 8 | *Full sun to partial shade. Well-drained, average garden soil. Prune plants back after flowering to maintain vigor and encourage a second bloom.* |
| | **CATNIP** *Nepeta cataria* | *A perennial member of the mint family bearing pairs of coarsely toothed, gray-green leaves and square stems. The ⅓-in., tubular, white flowers have 2 lips and are clustered at the ends of branches that grow off the stem.* | *Mid-summer to early autumn* | Height: 1–3' Spread: 6–18" | *Leaves used in cat treats and herbal teas.* | 3 to 10 | *Full sun to partial shade. Well-drained, average garden soil. Sow seeds or plant rooted cuttings. Prune plants back after flowering to maintain vigor. Harvest leaves in late summer. Cats digging up plants can be a problem.* |
| | **CAYENNE** CAYENNE PEPPER *Capsicum annuum* Longum group | *A tender perennial whose glossy, red, 1- to 2-in. fruits are ground to make a hot-pepper powder rich in vitamin C. Clusters of creamy white flowers, each with 5 pointed petals, are borne at the bases of the smooth, 2- to 6-in. leaves.* | *Summer* | Height: 1–2' Spread: 1–1½' | *Hot-pepper powder is ground from dried fruits and used in stews. For milder powder, discard seeds before grinding.* | 10 to 11 | *Full sun. Humus-rich, moist, well-drained soil. Start seeds indoors in early spring, setting plants out after last frost. Harvest fruits as they turn from green to red by pruning the stem. Grow cayenne as an annual north of zone 10.* |

◄ *Indicates species shown*

# Herbs for American Gardens

| | | | Time of Bloom | Height & Spread | Uses | Hardiness Zones | Growing Conditions |
|---|---|---|---|---|---|---|---|
| | **CHAMOMILE** ROMAN CHAMOMILE *Chamaemelum nobile* | A perennial herb whose flowers, with an applelike fragrance and flavor, have long been used for herbal teas. Daisylike, 1-in. flowers with yellow centers and white outer florets are borne on sprawling stems with downy, threadlike leaves. | Late spring to late summer | Height: 6–12" Spread: 6–12" | Flowers used in teas, salads, herbal baths, and hair rinses. Ornamental flowers and foliage. | 3 to 10 | Full sun to partial shade. Well-drained, sandy soil. Sow the fine seeds on the soil surface and keep moist until seedlings are established. Harvest flower heads as the outer petals start to curve back. |
| | **CHERVIL** *Anthriscus cerefolium* | An annual that resembles a delicate Queen-Anne's-lace. Pairs of soft, fernlike leaves have a mildly pungent fragrance. Small white flowers are borne in flat clusters at the tops of stems. | Late spring to mid-summer | Height: 1–2' Spread: 8–12" | Leaves used like parsley in soups, sauces, eggs, vegetables, and fish dishes; as a garnish; and in potpourris. | Hardy annual | Partial to full shade. Moist soil of average fertility. Sow seeds directly outdoors, ¼ in. deep, in early spring. Chervil does best in cool weather and can be grown as a container plant. Aphids may be a problem. |
| | **CHIVE** *Allium schoenoprasum* | A perennial herb grown for its tubular, onion-flavored leaves, which arise from tiny bulbs. Plants produce round clusters of lavender-pink, 6-petaled flowers on tough, leafless stems above clumps of foliage. | Late spring to mid-summer | Height: 6–18" Spread: 1–2' | Add leaves to salads, sauces, eggs, and vegetables (at end of cooking); use flowers in salads. Ornamental foliage and flowers. | 3 to 9 | Full sun to partial shade. Ordinary garden soil. Chive tolerates a wide variety of conditions. Grow from seed or divide clumps of bulbs. Harvest as needed; leaves regrow quickly. Use fresh or frozen; chive does not keep its flavor when dried. |
| | **CLARY** CLARY SAGE *Salvia sclarea* | A sage whose square stems and hairy leaves have a balsamic fragrance. The heart-shaped leaves are 6–9 in. long. Showy, 2-lipped, white, blue, or purple, ¾-in. flowers have pink bracts and form long spikes. | Early summer to mid-summer | Height: 3–5' Spread: 8–18" | Use fresh or dried leaves and flowers like sage in poultry, salads, and marinades. Leaves can be fried as a vegetable. Potpourri fixative. | 5 to 11 | Full sun. Sandy, well-drained soil of average fertility; avoid wet or damp soil. A biennial or short-lived perennial, clary can be grown as an annual or an indoor container plant north of zone 5. |
| | **COMFREY** *Symphytum officinale* | A perennial herb whose delightful light blue or pink, ½-in. flowers dangle from the tips of the shoots. The deep green, hairy, 6- to 10-in. leaves emerge from thick rhizomes. Leaves contain a suspected carcinogen and should not be ingested. | Mid-spring, periodically to late summer | Height: 2–4' Spread: 2–3' | Leaves and roots used in skin lotions and topical plasters. Ornamental leaves and flowers. | 3 to 11 | Full sun to partial shade. Moist, humus-rich soil. Plants spread from vigorous rhizomes and may be difficult to eradicate once established. Harvest leaves and roots, and use fresh as needed. |

| | | Time of Bloom | Height & Spread | Uses | Hardiness Zones | Growing Conditions |
|---|---|---|---|---|---|---|
| **CORIANDER**<br>CILANTRO<br>*Coriandrum sativum* | An annual herb whose compound leaves, called cilantro, are popular in Mexican and Asian cuisine. White or pink flowers in flat-topped clusters yield round, tan coriander seeds, with a citrusy fragrance. The flowers attract bees. | Mid-spring to mid-summer | Height: 2–3'<br>Spread: 6–12" | Fresh leaves and roots used in various cuisines. Dry seeds used in stews, vegetables, fruits, curries, fish, poultry, baked goods, and potpourris. | Half-hardy annual | Full sun to partial shade. Evenly moist, humus-rich, well-drained soil. Sow seeds ¼–½ in. deep after danger of frost has passed. Harvest leaves as needed and seeds just as tops start to wither. Dry seeds before using. |
| **COSTMARY**<br>*Chrysanthemum balsamita* var. *tanacetoides* | A perennial herb whose silvery green, hairy, 2- to 5-in.-long, tooth-edged leaves have a balsamic fragrance. The ¼-in., yellow flowers are clustered at the tops of shoots. Sometimes listed as Tanacetum balsamita. | Late summer | Height: 2–3'<br>Spread: 6–12" | Leaves used in beverages, salads, potpourris, skin lotions, and herbal baths. | 4 to 11 | Full sun to partial shade. Well-drained, humus-rich soil. Costmary grows best in dry, sunny locations. Propagate from cuttings or divisions, as seed production tends to be slight. |
| **DILL**<br>*Anethum graveolens* | A hardy annual whose ribbed, ⅛-in. seeds and finely divided, threadlike, blue-green leaves are used as culinary herbs. Erect, hollow stems are topped by flattened clusters of tiny yellow flowers that attract bees. | Mid-summer to early autumn | Height: 2–3'<br>Spread: 1–2' | Fresh or dried leaves used in salads or sauces and with fish, eggs, and poultry. Seeds and leaves used as pickling spices. | Hardy annual | Full sun. Moist, well-drained soil. Sow seeds ⅛ in. deep (they need light to germinate) at time of last frost, or start earlier indoors. Dill may self-sow in subsequent years. Aphids can be a problem. |
| **ELECAMPANE**<br>*Inula helenium* | A sturdy perennial whose roots are candied or used medicinally. The hairy stems and large, rough, dark green leaves with velvety undersides contrast with the 3- to 4-in., bright yellow, daisy-like flowers with very thin outer ray petals. | Summer | Height: 3–6'<br>Spread: 1–2' | Cooked roots eaten plain or candied and used for relief of chest colds and bronchial congestion. Ornamental flowers. | 3 to 9 | Full sun to partial shade. Moist, humus-rich soil. Elecampane grows best in damp loam with partial shade. Harvest roots in late summer to early autumn, and wait 2–3 years to harvest if the root is to be used medicinally. |
| **FENNEL**<br>◄ *Foeniculum vulgare*<br>FLORENCE FENNEL<br>*F. vulgare* var. *azoricum* | Perennials grown for their anise-flavored leaves and seeds. Florence fennel has swollen, clasping leaf bases that form a "bulb," eaten raw or cooked. An ornamental cultivar with bronze leaves is available. | Mid-summer to mid-autumn | Height: 3–4'<br>Spread: 1–2' | Dried seeds and fresh or frozen leaves used in salads, soups, and fish dishes (add near end of cooking since heat destroys the leaves' flavor). | 6 to 11<br>(Grow *F. vulgare* as an annual in zones 5–11) | Full sun. Sandy, fertile, well-drained, evenly moist, slightly alkaline soil. Sow seeds in mid-spring where plants are desired. Fennel grows most vigorously in warm weather and is grown as an annual when its seeds are the desired harvest. |

◄ *Indicates species shown*

# Herbs for American Gardens

| | | Time of Bloom | Height & Spread | Uses | Hardiness Zones | Growing Conditions |
|---|---|---|---|---|---|---|
| **FEVERFEW** <br> *Tanacetum parthenium* <br> *(Chrysanthemum parthenium)* | A perennial herb that was grown as a medicinal plant in colonial gardens. The bright green, fragrant, lobed foliage is adorned with abundant, 1-in., daisylike flowers comprised of stubby, white ray florets surrounding large yellow centers. | Mid-summer to early autumn | Height: 1–3' <br><br> Spread: 8–15" | Leaves used in anti-inflamma-tory and anal-gesic teas, as an insect repellent, and to produce a yellow-green dye. Ornamen-tal flowers. | 3 to 10 | Full sun to light shade. Humus-rich, well-drained soil. Feverfew may become weedy through self-seeding in soil that is con-stantly moist. Treat it as an annual in zone 3; provide winter mulch in zones 4–6. |
| **FOXGLOVE** <br> *Digitalis purpurea* | A biennial that produces rosettes of thick, soft leaves the first year. Second-year flower stalks bear many pink or white, tubular flowers, each decorated with con-trasting dots. Foxglove self-seeds so freely it may appear to be perennial. | Late spring to mid-summer | Height: 2–5' <br><br> Spread: 10–12" | Leaves con-tain a pow-erful heart stimulant that can be toxic. Ornamental flowers and foliage. | 4 to 8 | Full sun to partial shade. Moist, well-drained soil. Foxglove self-seeds, but not always where you desire it; transplant seedlings in the fall or early spring. Few pests bother the leaves, the source of the heart drug digitalis. |
| **GARLIC** <br> *Allium sativum* | A perennial, bulb-producing herb grown for its pungent bulb sections (cloves), which are covered by white, papery skins. Flat, grasslike leaves clasp the tough stems, which bear clusters of small white flowers. | Late spring to summer | Height: 1½–2' <br><br> Spread: 5–6" | Taken medici-nally as a curative and preventive. Culinary uses include sauces, salads, pasta, pickles, vegetables, and poultry. | 6 to 8 | Full sun. Moderately moist, well-drained soil that is not too rich in nutrients. If the soil is too fertile, most of the growth goes into the tops rather than the cloves. Harvest mature cloves; store in a cool (not refrigerated), well-ventilated area. |
| **GARLIC CHIVE** <br> CHINESE CHIVE <br> *Allium tuberosum* | A perennial herb grown for its flattened, dark green, 1-ft.-long leaves, which have a garlicky chive flavor. Rose-scented, 6-part, white flowers form 2-in. clusters. The elongated bulbs are covered with a fibrous, netlike skin. | Late summer | Height: 1–2' <br><br> Spread: 1–1½' | Add minced leaves to salads, sauces, eggs, and veg-etables (at end of cooking). Use flowers in salads. Orna-mental foliage and flowers. | 7 to 11 | Full sun to partial shade. Ordinary garden soil. Gar-lic chive tolerates a variety of conditions. Grow from seed or divide clumps of bulbs. Harvest as needed; leaves regrow quickly. Use fresh or frozen; it loses flavor when dried. |
| **GERMANDER** <br> *Teucrium chamaedrys* | A shrubby perennial with dense masses of small (⅓–½ in.), hairy, aromatic leaves. Germander is grown more for its foliage than for the small spikes of ½-in., red-dish purple, 2-lipped flowers. | Late summer to early autumn | Height: 8–12" <br><br> Spread: 6–12" | Leaves used in astringent skin lotions, wound healers, and potpourris. Ornamental foliage; good for knot gardens. | 4 to 10 | Full sun to partial shade. Well-drained, sandy loam. Propagate plants from cut-tings, as seeds are very slow to germinate. Ger-mander makes an excellent low hedge for herb and rock gardens. |

| | | Time of Bloom | Height & Spread | Uses | Hardiness Zones | Growing Conditions |
|---|---|---|---|---|---|---|
| **GOLDENROD** ◀ *Solidago* spp. SWEET GOLDENROD *S. odora* | Perennial plants with golden yellow, $1/4$- to $1/3$-in. flowers in sprays or spikes at the tops of somewhat woody stems. S. odora has anise-scented leaves. Dwarf varieties that reach only a few inches high are available. | Late summer to early autumn | Height: 1–5' Spread: 1–1½' | Leaves and flowers used in astringent skin lotions. Ornamental flowers produce yellow dye. Leaves and flowers of S. odora used in herbal teas. | 4 to 9 | Full sun. Well-drained soil of average to poor fertility. S. odora is clump-forming and spreads slowly. Goldenrods are often confused with the hay-fever-inducing ragweeds (genus Ambrosia), but their pollen is not an allergen. |
| **HOP** *Humulus lupulus* | A perennial vine that climbs by twining its stems around supports. Attractive, grape-like, rough-surfaced leaves have 3–5 deep lobes and long stems. Flowers are borne in dangling clusters that produce sacklike fruits arranged in cones. | Summer | Height: 10–25' Spread: 12–18' | Female flowers used to flavor and preserve beers and ales. Ornamental vines. | 3 to 11 | Full sun. Deep, well-drained soil rich in humus. Plant seeds where desired in mid-spring, and provide support for vines to twine around. Plants may self-sow or become weedy in subsequent years. Downy mildew can be a problem. |
| **HOREHOUND** *Marrubium vulgare* | A bushy perennial with soft, woolly, rounded, 2-in. leaves and square stems that indicate its membership in the mint family. Dense whorls of small white flowers attract bees. | Summer | Height: 1½–3' Spread: 12–15" | Leaves used for cough syrup and sore throat soother; candy made from leaf infusion. Ornamental foliage in herb garden. | 4 to 11 | Full sun. Deep, sandy, well-drained soil. Horehound grows easily and can become weedy if not trimmed back before seed sets. Plants from seed produce flowers after second year. Divide plants every several years. |
| **HORSERADISH** *Armoracia rusticana* | A perennial grown mainly for its white, fleshy, sharply pungent taproots, which are grated and used as a condiment or seasoning. Young leaves can be used in salads. The older leaves become large (1–2 ft.) and tough. | Summer | Height: 2–2½' Spread: 1–1½' | Grate fresh root to season meat, poultry, and fish. Young greens can be used in salads. Ground root is used in muscle compresses. | 3 to 11 | Full sun. Well-drained, nutrient-rich soil. Propagate from root cuttings in early spring; replanting sections of lateral root works well. Harvest horseradish roots in autumn, when cool weather brings peak flavor. |
| **HORSETAIL** SCOURING RUSH *Equisetum hyemale* | An evergreen perennial with hollow, jointed stems that are coated with silica. The light green color of the stems deepens during winter. Spores are produced in a conelike structure at the top of the shoot. E. hyemale has no leaves. | Produces spores (cones) instead of flowers in mid-spring | Height: 1–4' Spread: 1–3' | Stems used as an abrasive and for a yellow-green wool dye. Ornamental foliage. | 4 to 10 | Full sun to partial shade. Wet, humus-rich soil. Horsetail will grow well in water up to 6 in. deep. Plants spread with age from vigorous rhizomes. Grow them in pots or open-bottomed containers to keep under control. |

◀ Indicates species shown

# Herbs for American Gardens

| | | Time of Bloom | Height & Spread | Uses | Hardiness Zones | Growing Conditions |
|---|---|---|---|---|---|---|
| **HYSSOP** *Hyssopus officinalis* | A square-stemmed perennial herb clothed in pairs of 1- to 1¹/₂-in., smooth, pointed leaves with the fragrance of camphor and a mintlike flavor. The clusters of blue, white, or violet, ¹/₃- to ¹/₂-in., 2-lipped, tubular flowers attract bees. | Mid- to late summer | Height: 1¹/₂–2' Spread: 9–15" | Leaves and flowers used sparingly in salads, soups, herbal teas, and herbal baths; also to flavor liqueurs. | 5 to 11 | Full sun to partial shade. Sandy, well-drained, alkaline soil. Propagate plants from seeds or cuttings, or divide roots in spring and autumn. |
| **INDIGO** FRENCH INDIGO *Indigofera tinctoria* | A tropical shrub grown for the blue dye produced by fermenting its leaves. Cylindrical clusters of small, red-and-yellow, pealike flowers emerge from the bases of compound leaves that bear 7–15 oblong leaflets. | Late summer | Height: 2–5' Spread: 3–5' | Blue dye made from fermented leaves. | 10 to 11 | Full sun. Humus-rich, evenly moist, well-drained soil. Indigo is very frost sensitive. It can be grown as a greenhouse plant. |
| **LADY'S-MANTLE** *Alchemilla vulgaris* ◀ *(A. mollis)* | A perennial with attractive scalloped, gray-green foliage exuding water droplets that remain on the leaves most of the day. Tiny yellow-green flowers are borne in loose, spraylike clusters above the leaves. Leaves and flowers have no scent. | Spring to mid-summer | Height: 8–18" Spread: 1–2' | Flowers used in fresh or dried arrangements. Ornamental foliage and flowers. | 4 to 8 | Full sun to partial shade. Lady's-mantle prefers ordinary garden conditions—loamy soil and even moisture. It does not grow well in very wet or very dry soil. Plants can become somewhat weedy with age and may need to be divided. |
| **LAVENDER** ENGLISH LAVENDER *Lavandula angustifolia* | A genus of perennial herbs grown for their attractive, exquisitely scented, purple flowers. English lavender, the most familiar species, has the strongest fragrance. Its flowers bloom in slender 6- to 8-in. spikes. The foliage is silvery grayish green. | Late spring to early summer | Height: 2–3' Spread: 1¹/₂–2' | Flowers used in potpourris, cosmetics, soaps, perfumes, herbal baths, and insect repellents. Ornamental flowers and foliage. | 5 to 8 | Full sun. Sandy or stony, well-drained soil. Harvest flowers just before they open, and immediately dry them for storage. Plants need protection where winters are harsh. |
| **LAVENDER** FRENCH LAVENDER *Lavandula dentata* | A shrubby lavender with smaller, less pungent spikes of light purple flowers than L. angustifolia. The densely woolly, gray-green, fernlike leaves have blunt-toothed edges and are ¹/₂–³/₄ in. long. | Early spring to late summer | Height: 1–4' Spread: 1–2' | Flowers used in potpourris, cosmetics, soaps, perfumes, herbal baths, and insect repellents. Ornamental flowers and foliage. | 8 to 11 | Full sun. Sandy or stony, well-drained soil. Harvest flowers just before they open, and immediately dry them for storage. North of zone 8, grow French lavender as an indoor plant over winter. |

| | | | Time of Bloom | Height & Spread | Uses | Hardiness Zones | Growing Conditions |
|---|---|---|---|---|---|---|---|
| | **LAVENDER** SPANISH LAVENDER *Lavandula stoechas* | The mildest of the lavenders, native to Spain and Portugal. This species has small, ³/₄- to 1¹/₄-in. spikes of deep purple flowers at the tips of shoots. The woolly gray leaves may reach 1 in. long. | Late spring to early summer | Height: 1–2' Spread: 6–12" | Flowers used in potpourris, cosmetics, soaps, perfumes, herbal baths, and insect repellents. Ornamental flowers and foliage. | 8 to 11 | Full sun. Sandy or stony, well-drained soil. Harvest flowers just before they open, and immediately dry them for storage. Plants need protection where winters are harsh. |
| | **LAVENDER COTTON** *Santolina chamaecyparissus* | A perennial shrub whose silvery gray leaves have a musky lavender scent. The 1¹/₄-in., divided, evergreen leaves give the branch tips a knobby effect. Tiny yellow flowers are clustered into ¹/₃- to ¹/₂-in., buttonlike heads. | Late spring to early summer | Height: 1¹/₂–2' Spread: 6–12" | Leaves used in astringent skin lotions, potpourris, and sachets to repel insects. Flowers used in dried arrangements. Ornamental foliage. | 6 to 8 | Full sun. Sandy, alkaline, well-drained soil of poor or average fertility. Plants may die over winter in wet, cold soil. Lavender cotton may be pruned into an ornamental low hedge in the herb garden. |
| | **LEMON BALM** *Melissa officinalis* | A member of the mint family with 1- to 3-in., pebble-surfaced leaves that combine lemon and mint fragrances. The small white flowers at the bases of the leaves attract bees. | Mid- to late summer | Height: 1¹/₂–2' Spread: 1¹/₂–2' | Fresh or dried leaves used in herbal teas, beverages, potpourris, and skin cleansers. Add fresh leaves to salads, fruits, and vegetables. | 4 to 7 | Full sun to partial shade. Average, evenly moist, well-drained soil. Harvest leaves before plants flower to increase production, and dry them quickly. Plants spread with time. Powdery mildew can be a problem. |
| | **LEMONGRASS** *Cymbopogon citratus* | A tender perennial grass whose soft, bright green foliage is a commercial source of lemon oil. The evergreen leaves, 2–3 ft. long and 1–1¹/₂ in. wide, grow in dense clumps. | Late summer | Height: 3–4' Spread: 2–3' | Leaves used in Thai and Vietnamese dishes. | 9 to 11 | Full sun to light shade. Moist, well-drained, humus-rich soil. Sow seeds or plant rootstock divisions in midspring. Plants are drought tolerant once established. Lemongrass grows best in warm weather; grow as an annual north of zone 9. |
| | **LEMON VERBENA** *Aloysia triphylla* | A frost-sensitive, somewhat woody perennial shrub with 2- to 3-in.-long, ¹/₂- to 1-in.-wide, light green leaves with a lemony fragrance. Leaves are arranged in whorls of 4, from which spikes of tiny lavender flowers emerge. | Late summer to early autumn | Height: 3–8' Spread: 1–2' | Leaves used in herbal teas, potpourris, perfumes, skin lotions, and herbal baths. | 9 to 11 | Full sun. Moist, humus-rich, well-drained soil of high fertility. Harvest leaves in midsummer and again in autumn. Lemon verbena can be grown as an annual or a potted plant north of zone 9. Spider mites and whiteflies can be problems. |

◄ *Indicates species shown*

# Herbs for American Gardens

| | | Time of Bloom | Height & Spread | Uses | Hardiness Zones | Growing Conditions |
|---|---|---|---|---|---|---|
| **LOVAGE** <br> *Levisticum officinale* | A tall perennial herb whose glossy, medium green, toothed leaves have a peppery flavor that tastes of celery and parsley. The flat-topped, 3-in. clusters of tiny yellow flowers and the ribbed stems also have a celery-like flavor. | Late spring to early summer | Height: 4–6' <br><br> Spread: 2–3' | Use chopped stems and leaves to flavor stews, salads, soups, poultry, and sauces. All parts once used as a folk remedy for stomachaches. | 3 to 7 | Full sun to partial shade in humus-rich, well-drained, evenly moist soil. Grows best in partial shade in warm climates. Harvest leaves as needed and use fresh or dry. Leaf miners and aphids may be problems. |
| **MARJORAM** <br> SWEET MARJORAM <br> *Origanum majorana* | A close relative of oregano, with a milder flavor and fragrance. The fuzzy, pale gray-green, 1/4- to 1-in. leaves and the spikes of small white, pink, or purple flowers of this frost-sensitive perennial can be used fresh or dried. | Late summer to early autumn | Height: 8–16" <br><br> Spread: 4–8" | Use fresh or dried leaves and flowers to flavor meat, poultry, and vegetable dishes. Dried flowers and leaves used in potpourris. | 9 to 11 | Full sun. Sandy, well-drained, average soil. Start seeds indoors in early spring and plant outdoors after last frost. Root rot and fungal diseases can be a problem if soil is too wet. |
| **MARSH MALLOW** <br> *Althaea officinalis* | An erect perennial whose taproots were once used to make the puffy confection that bears its name. The 1- to 2-in., pinkish white, hollyhock-like flowers are borne at the bases of the roundish, hairy, gray-green leaves. | Midsummer to early autumn | Height: 3–5' <br><br> Spread: 1–2' | Mucilaginous extract of roots used as a digestive aid and to make confections. Very young leaves can be added to salads. | 6 to 9 | Full sun. Moist, humus-rich, well-drained soil; sandy loam is best. Harvest taproots in autumn from plants that are at least 2 years old. |
| **MINT** <br> PEPPERMINT <br> *Mentha × piperita* <br> BERGAMOT MINT, <br> ORANGE MINT <br> *M. × piperita* var. *citrata* | Strong-flavored perennial herbs. Peppermint is the classic mint and a commercial source of menthol. The square purple stems bear 1- to 2½-in. leaves. Orange mint's leaves, mottled with purple, exude a citrus odor when crushed. | Summer | Height: 1–3' <br><br> Spread: 1–3' | Fresh or dried leaves used as a digestive aid or flavoring agent and in herbal teas, salads, potpourris, and skin cleansers. | 4 to 11 | Full sun to partial shade. Moist, humus-rich, well-drained soil. Harvest young leaves as needed and use fresh or dry. Plants may spread aggressively from runners. Grow in bottomless pots to control spread. Leaf rust may be a problem. |
| **MINT** <br> CORSICAN MINT, <br> CREME-DE-MENTHE <br> PLANT <br> *Mentha requienii* | A low-growing mint whose 1/4- to 1/2-in., bright green, rounded leaves have a very strong mint fragrance and flavor. The smooth stems creep along the ground and bear lavender flowers. | Summer | Height: 1–4" <br><br> Spread: 1–2' | Leaves used in herbal teas and to flavor liqueur. | 6 to 11 | Full sun to partial shade. Humus-rich, moist soil. Corsican mint is not very aggressive, spreading slowly with age. |

| | | Time of Bloom | Height & Spread | Uses | Hardiness Zones | Growing Conditions |
|---|---|---|---|---|---|---|
| **MINT**<br>SPEARMINT<br>*Mentha spicata* | *A strong-flavored mint, milder than peppermint. Pairs of toothed, pointed, 2-in., lance-shaped leaves clasp the square stems. The small flowers range in color from white to pink to lilac.* | Summer | Height: 1½–3'<br><br>Spread: 1–3' | Leaves used in herbal teas, salads, sauces, soups, and with meat and vegetables. | 3 to 11 | Full sun to partial shade. Moist, humus-rich, well-drained soil. Harvest young leaves as needed and use fresh or dry. Plants may spread aggressively from runners. Grow in bottomless pots to control spread. Leaf rust may be a problem. |
| **MINT**<br>APPLE MINT<br>*Mentha suaveolens* | *A mint whose soft, hairy, 1- to 4-in., rounded leaves have a mild fruity flavor reminiscent of apples. Its flowers are pink to white.* | Summer | Height: 1–2'<br><br>Spread: 1–2' | Fresh or dried leaves used in drinks and salads or with fruits. | 6 to 11 | Full sun to partial shade. Moist, humus-rich, well-drained soil. Harvest young leaves as needed and use fresh or dry. Leaf rust may be a problem. |
| **MINT MARIGOLD**<br>MEXICAN MINT,<br>MARIGOLDSWEET,<br>SCENTED MARIGOLD<br>*Tagetes lucida* | *A frost-sensitive perennial marigold with a few small, fragrant, yellow flowers clustered in heads ¼–½ in. wide. Pairs of elongated, lance-shaped, pungent leaves attach directly to the stems.* | Late summer to mid-autumn | Height: 1–2'<br><br>Spread: 6–12" | Leaves used as a substitute for tarragon in soups, stews, vinegars, and sauces, and with fish, shellfish, eggs, and poultry. | 10 to 11 | Full sun. Evenly moist, well-drained, humus-rich soil. Mint marigold can be grown as a container plant indoors during winter or as an annual. Start seeds indoors 4 weeks before the last frost. |
| **MUGWORT**<br>*Artemisia vulgaris* | *A perennial in the wormwood family with deeply cut, 4-in., pungent leaves that are smooth and dark green above, but woolly white below. Reddish brown flowers are clustered in ⅓-in., oval heads at ends of hairy, purple branches.* | Summer | Height: 4–6'<br><br>Spread: 1½–2' | Leaves used as moth repellent and in herbal baths. Ornamental foliage. | 3 to 11 | Full sun. Well-drained soil of poor to average fertility, kept on the dry side. Harvest leaves in midsummer and dry them in the shade. Plants spread slowly by rhizomes. |
| **MULLEIN**<br>COMMON MULLEIN,<br>FLANNEL PLANT<br>*Verbascum thapsus* | *A biennial with striking 4- to 12-in., fuzzy, gray-green leaves that grow in a low rosette the first year. The second year a long, wandlike stem emerges bearing 1-in., 5-petaled yellow flowers.* | Late spring to late summer | Height: 3–6'<br><br>Spread: 1–2' | Flowers used in herbal teas for congestion and sore throat. Ornamental foliage and flowers. | 3 to 8 | Full sun. Well-drained soil of average fertility. Mullein grows best in sandy soil. It is prone to root rot if soil is too wet. |

◁ *Indicates species shown*

# Herbs for American Gardens

| | | Time of Bloom | Height & Spread | Uses | Hardiness Zones | Growing Conditions |
|---|---|---|---|---|---|---|
| **MUSTARD**<br>BROWN MUSTARD<br>*Brassica juncea*<br>BLACK MUSTARD<br>◄ *B. nigra* | Annuals with branched stems, bright yellow, 4-petaled flowers, and aromatic leaves and seeds. B. nigra has black seeds used for making pungent yellow mustards, while B. juncea is preferred for salad greens and has milder-tasting seeds. | Early summer | B. juncea Height: 2–4' Spread: 9–18"<br><br>B. nigra Height: 4–6' Spread: 1–2' | Use leaves as salad or cooking greens. Use seeds in mustards, pickles, and sauces, or in analgesic plasters to relieve bronchial congestion. | Half-hardy annual | Full sun. Humus-rich, well-drained soil. Sow seeds $1/8$ in. deep in early spring. Harvest seeds when pods turn from green to tan; harvest leaves when young and tender. Plants self-sow and become weedy. |
| **MYRTLE**<br>*Myrtus communis* | A shrubby, evergreen perennial with strongly scented, 2-in., blue-green leaves. In the past myrtle was used as a culinary herb but has been found to be toxic. The $3/4$-in., 4-petaled, fragrant white flowers produce $1/2$-in., blue-black fruits. | Late spring to early autumn | Height: 5–10' Spread: 4–7' | Ornamental, fragrant foliage and stems. | 9 to 11 | Full sun to partial shade. Humus-rich, evenly moist, well-drained soil. Myrtle can be grown as a potted plant. |
| **NASTURTIUM**<br>*Tropaeolum majus* | A garden favorite, grown for its showy flowers and attractive foliage, both of which are edible. The 2- to 3-in., spurred flowers are usually yellow or orange, often spotted or streaked with red. Both trailing vine and dwarf bush forms are available. | Summer to frost | Height: 1–10' Spread: 1–10' | Fresh leaves, flowers, and flower buds used in salads. Buds can be pickled like capers. Ornamental flowers and foliage. | Tender annual | Full sun to partial shade. Average, well-drained soil. For abundant flowers do not add fertilizer. Sow seeds directly where plants are desired after all danger of frost has passed. Nasturtium grows best in cool weather. |
| **ONION**<br>*Allium cepa* | Popular perennial grown for its pungent bulbs and hollow, green, succulent stems. Plants produce attractive round clusters of white or pink, $1/3$-in. flowers. Cultivars range from mild-tasting Bermuda onions to sharply flavored top onions. | Summer | Height: 1–4' Spread: 6–12" | Leaves and bulbs used in salads, soups, sauces, and with meat and poultry. Bulb skins yield yellow, tan, and orange dyes. | 4 to 10 | Full sun. Humus-rich, evenly moist, well-drained soil; plants do not tolerate soggy conditions. Raise from seeds or small bulbs ("sets"). When tops start to yellow, break stems over and allow to wither. Dig up bulbs before ground freezes. |
| **OREGANO**<br>GREEK OREGANO<br>*Origanum heracleoticum*<br>GOLDEN OREGANO<br>◄ *O. vulgare 'Aureum'* | Favorite herbs for Italian cuisine. The 2-in. leaves are pointed; those of golden oregano are yellow. The $1/4$-in., 2-lipped, lavender to white flowers are clustered at the tops of square stems. Greek oregano has the best flavor. | Mid- to late summer | Height: 1–2' Spread: 1–2' | Dried or fresh leaves used to flavor sauces, eggs, tomatoes, pizza, pasta, and cheese. Ornamental foliage. | 5 to 11 | Full sun. Sandy, well-drained soil of average fertility. Propagate plants from cuttings, as seeds often vary from their parental stock. Oregano can be grown as a houseplant. Root rot and fungal diseases can be problems in wet soil. |

| | | | Time of Bloom | Height & Spread | Uses | Hardiness Zones | Growing Conditions |
|---|---|---|---|---|---|---|---|
| | **ORRIS**<br>FLAG<br>*Iris × germanica* var. *florentina* | A rhizomatous perennial with beautiful white flowers veined in purple and bearing white beards. The rhizomes of this iris are harvested for their violet-like scent, which develops as the dried rootstocks age. | Late spring | Height: 2–2½'<br><br>Spread: 1–1½' | Dried rhizomes used in potpourris and sachets. Ornamental foliage and flowers. | 5 to 11 | Full sun. Humus-rich, well-drained, evenly moist soil. Divide rhizomes every several years to promote vigorous growth and abundant flowering. Root rot may be a problem. |
| | **PARSLEY**<br>*Petroselinum crispum* | A biennial herb grown as an annual in the garden or in pots for its deep green, pungent foliage. Several varieties differ in the amount of leaf curliness. Plants lose flavor in their second year. | Summer | Height: 6–12"<br><br>Spread: 6–12" | Leaves used in salads, vegetables, or sauces; with poultry; and in herbal baths, skin lotions, soaps, and shampoos. | Very hardy annual | Full sun to partial shade. Moist, well-drained soil of average fertility. Soak seeds in water overnight to hasten germination. Harvest leaves by picking them rather than by uprooting plants. Parsley can be brought indoors for the winter. |
| | **PENNYROYAL**<br>*Mentha pulegium* | A square-stemmed perennial mint whose pairs of ½-in., rounded, hairy leaves have a minty fragrance. The ¼-in., lilac flowers are densely clustered around the bases of the leaves. The sprawling stems form a dense ground cover. | Late summer | Height: 4–12"<br><br>Spread: 1–2' | Leaves used in herbal teas and as insect repellent. Ornamental ground cover. | 5 to 11 | Full sun to partial shade. Humus-rich, moist soil. Plants spread rapidly. |
| | **PERILLA**<br>*Perilla frutescens* | A branched, shrubby annual whose pairs of pointed, 5-in., anise-flavored leaves have a purplish or greenish metallic sheen. Lavender, pink, or white flowers are borne at the tops of hairy shoots. | Early autumn | Height: 1½–3'<br><br>Spread: 6–18" | Fresh leaves and seeds used to flavor herbal teas, salads, and rice dishes. Ornamental foliage provides contrast to other herbs. | Half-hardy annual | Full sun to partial shade. Humus-rich, well-drained soil. Sow seeds ⅛–¼ in. deep in mid-spring, or start indoors in early spring. They need light to germinate. Harvest leaves as needed. |
| | **ROSE**<br>DAMASK ROSE<br>*Rosa damascena*<br>RUGOSA ROSE<br>◀ *R. rugosa* | Old-fashioned shrubby roses bearing a succession of large (3½-in.), fragrant magenta, red, or pink flowers with gold centers. Damask roses are prized for their fragrance; rugosa roses produce tomato-shaped fruits (hips), high in vitamin C. | Early summer to early autumn | Height: 3–6'<br><br>Spread: 1–3' | Damask rose petals, rich in rose oil, candied or used in cosmetics, skin lotions, or potpourri. Rose hips used in teas, jellies, and vitamins. | R. damasc: 5 to 9<br><br>R. rugosa: 3 to 9 | Full sun to light shade. Well-drained soil with ample moisture and organic matter. R. rugosa tolerates windy and salty environments and is one of the best roses for seaside plantings. |

◀ Indicates species shown

# Herbs for American Gardens

| | | Time of Bloom | Height & Spread | Uses | Hardiness Zones | Growing Conditions |
|---|---|---|---|---|---|---|
| **ROSEMARY** *Rosmarinus officinalis* | A tender perennial evergreen shrub with scaly gray bark and pairs of needlelike, ³/₄-in. leaves, dark green above and pale below. Plants come in prostrate and upright forms; cultivars have different foliage and flower colors. | Early summer | Height: 4–5' Spread: 3–6' | Fresh or dried leaves used to flavor meat, poultry, soups, and sauces. Leaves used in herbal baths and astringent skin lotions. | 8 to 11 | Full sun to partial shade. Deep, sandy, well-drained soil. Propagate plants from cuttings. North of zone 8 grow rosemary as an annual or in a large pot to hold its extensive roots. Scale insects and mealybugs can be problems. |
| **RUE** *Ruta graveolens* | An evergreen shrub at one time believed to have magical powers, now grown as an ornamental for its yellow flower clusters and 3- to 5-in., lacy, blue-green leaves. Some people develop skin rashes from contact. It has a pungent aroma. | Late spring to mid-summer | Height: 2–3' Spread: 1¹/₂–2' | Ornamental waxy, blue-green foliage and small yellow flowers. | 5 to 9 | Full sun. Well-drained, clay-loam soil. Rue is prone to fungal diseases in warm, wet weather. |
| **SAFFRON** *Crocus sativus* | A perennial autumn-blooming crocus that yields one of the most expensive of all spices. The fragrant, 2- to 3-in., white or lavender flowers have 6 petallike parts and produce blood-red stigmas harvested for spices and dyes. | Early autumn | Height: 1–1¹/₂' Spread: 6–9" | Dried stigmas add color and flavor to rice, breads, cakes, vegetables, and soups. Ground stigmas yield deep yellow dye. Ornamental flowers. | 6 to 10 | Full sun to partial shade. Well-drained, sandy soil. Plant bulbs (corms) in spring or fall. Harvest stigmas as outer petals start to curve back; dry on a piece of paper and store in sealed vials. |
| **SAGE** PINEAPPLE-SCENTED SAGE *Salvia elegans* | A frost-sensitive sage whose 2- to 4-in., hairy, toothed, oval leaves have a distinctive pineapple scent. The 2-lipped, red, tubular, 1¹/₂-in. flowers are quite striking and attract hummingbirds to the garden. | Late winter to early spring | Height: 2–3' Spread: 1¹/₂–2' | Leaves used in beverages and with poultry and cheese. Ornamental flowers. | 10 to 11 | Full sun. Humus-rich, well-drained soil. North of zone 10 grow pineapple sage as an annual or a container plant, giving it a sunny spot in winter. Wilt, root rot, and spider mites can be problems. |
| **SAGE** COMMON SAGE *Salvia officinalis* | A hardy perennial with somewhat shrubby, square, downy stems that bear pairs of 1- to 2-in., gray-green leaves. Flowers are pink, white, or lavender. Sage is the classic herb for seasoning poultry and dressing. | Late spring | Height: 1–2¹/₂' Spread: 1–2' | Leaves used to season poultry, eggs, meat, vegetables, and salads, and in lotions and cosmetics. Ornamental foliage and flowers. | 4 to 8 | Full sun. Humus-rich, well-drained soil. Sage can be grown indoors as a container plant in a sunny spot over winter. Wilt, root rot, and spider mites can be problems. |

| | | | Time of Bloom | Height & Spread | Uses | Hardiness Zones | Growing Conditions |
|---|---|---|---|---|---|---|---|
| | **SALAD BURNET**<br>*Poterium sanguisorba* | A sprawling perennial whose long leafstalks bear pairs of toothed, smooth, gray-green leaflets with a cucumber scent. The clusters of small, 5-petaled, reddish flowers rise above the leaves. | Mid-spring to late spring | Height: 1–3'<br><br>Spread: 8–15" | Tender young leaves used in salads or drinks and as a garnish. Ornamental foliage and flowers. | 3 to 11 | Full sun to partial shade. Well-drained, alkaline, evenly moist soil. Burnet responds well to additions of ground limestone. Plants are prone to root rot in wet soils. |
| | **SAVORY**<br>SUMMER SAVORY<br>*Satureja hortensis* | An annual plant with a milder taste than winter savory. Pairs of soft, smooth, 1-in., grayish leaves curl under at the edges. White, pink, or lavender flowers, $1/4$ in. long, grow at the leaf bases. | Mid-summer to frost | Height: 6–18"<br><br>Spread: 1–2' | Leaves used in herbal teas, soups, sauces, vinegars, and herb butters. | Half-hardy annual | Full sun. Average, well-drained soil. Start seeds indoors, $1/8$ in. deep, in early spring; transplant outdoors after danger of frost has passed. Harvest leaves as needed. Summer savory may self-sow in warm regions. |
| | **SAVORY**<br>WINTER SAVORY<br>*Satureja montana* | A semievergreen, compact perennial with a bushy form. The glossy, dark green, 1-in., lance-shaped leaves have a pungent, resinous scent. Pink, lilac, or white, $1/3$-in. flowers are borne in spikes at the branch tips. | Mid-summer to early autumn | Height: 6–12"<br><br>Spread: 1–1$1/2$' | Chop dried or fresh leaves to season game, meat, and vegetables. Ornamental foliage; low hedge or herb garden border plant. | 6 to 11 | Full sun. Sandy, well-drained soil. Harvest leaves in summer and use fresh or dry. North of zone 9, winter savory can be grown as an annual or brought indoors during winter. Root rot may be a problem, especially in damp soil. |
| | **SCENTED GERANIUM**<br>ROSE GERANIUM<br>*Pelargonium graveolens*<br>APPLE GERANIUM<br>*P. odoratissimum* | Frost-sensitive plants whose soft, velvety leaves release delightful fragrances when rubbed. Apple geranium has sprawling branches with small leaves and white flowers. Rose geranium has dissected leaves and rosy pink or red flower petals. | Summer | Height: 1–2'<br><br>Spread: 1–2' | Leaves used to flavor herbal teas and in potpourris and sachets. Ornamental foliage and flowers. | 10 to 11 | Full sun to partial shade. Average soil. Grow scented geraniums as annuals north of zone 10. Propagate from cuttings, or start seeds indoors (provide bottom heat) 10–12 weeks before last frost. Both species grow best with cool nights. |
| | **SHALLOT**<br>MULTIPLIER ONION<br>*Allium cepa*<br>Aggregatum group | A delicate-flavored onion, important in French cuisine. Shallots develop a cluster of small brown bulbs, topped by tubular leaves that can be used as scallions. | Summer | Height: 1–2'<br><br>Spread: 3–6" | Use chopped leaves as scallions; use bulbs as mild onions. | 5 to 11 | Full sun. Fertile, well-drained soil. Plant small bulbs ("sets") in mid-spring. When tops start to yellow, break the stems over and allow to wither. Dig up bulbs before ground freezes. Save small ones for sets. |

◄ *Indicates species shown*

# Herbs for American Gardens

| | | Time of Bloom | Height & Spread | Uses | Hardiness Zones | Growing Conditions |
|---|---|---|---|---|---|---|
| **SORREL** *Rumex acetosa* FRENCH SORREL *R. scutatus* | Perennials with 6-in., lance-shaped leaves that grow in thick clumps. If not cut back, flowers rise on stems 2–3 feet above foliage. The tangy leaves are used as a mild seasoning for soups and salads. | Late spring | Height: 1–4' Spread: 6–12" | Fresh leaves used to season salads, soups, sauces, or lamb, or as cooked greens. | 5 to 9 | Full sun to light shade. Average garden soil. Sow seeds outdoors in early spring. Do not allow plants to flower. Harvest young leaves as needed, periodically cutting stems back to the ground to encourage growth of new leaves. |
| **SOUTHERN-WOOD** *Artemisia abrotanum* | A perennial in the worm-wood family whose finely divided, downy, gray-green leaves have a citrusy fragrance. Light yellow flowers are clustered in 1/6-in., nodding, globular heads. Plants may remain evergreen where winters are mild. | Late summer | Height: 3–5' Spread: 2–3' | Leaves used as insect repellent, in herbal baths, and to produce a yellow dye. Ornamental foliage. | 4 to 8 | Full sun. Average, well-drained soil. Prune in early spring to shape shrub and stimulate vigorous growth. Aphids may be a problem. |
| **SWEET CICELY** *Myrrhis odorata* | A perennial herb whose broadly triangular, ferny leaves, covered with fine white hairs, have the aroma of celery when crushed. The 2-in. umbels of small white flowers produce many 1-in.-long, dark, ribbed seeds with an anise flavor. | Mid-spring to late spring | Height: 1–3' Spread: 1–2' | Fresh leaves used in salads and with vegetables. Roots cooked as vegetables. Seeds used to flavor candy or liqueur. | 4 to 8 | Partial to full shade. Humus-rich, moist, well-drained soil. Harvest fresh leaves as needed and seeds as they start to darken. |
| **SWEET FLAG** *Acorus calamus* | A perennial of the arum family with 2- to 4-ft., swordlike leaves, each with a single rib down its length. Both the leaves and the 2-in., coblike cluster of yellow-green flowers are fragrant. A cultivar is available with yellow-striped leaves. | Late spring to late summer | Height: 3–4' Spread: 1–2' | Ornamental foliage. Cinnamon-scented leaves can be used in potpourris. Possible carcinogen; not to be used as culinary or medicinal herb. | 4 to 11 | Full sun to partial shade. Sweet flag grows best in waterlogged soil or in shallow ponds, but is adaptable to upland soils, except those that dry out completely. Plantings benefit from the division of rhizomes every few years. |
| **SWEET WOODRUFF** *Galium odoratum* | An easy-to-grow perennial ground cover traditionally used to flavor wine. The 1- to 2-in. leaves are arranged in whorls of 6–8 around the square stems. Cross-shaped, 1/3-in., white flowers are borne in loose clusters above the foliage. | Spring | Height: 8–12" Spread: 6–12" | Fresh leaves used to flavor May wine. Dried leaves used in potpourris. Ornamental foliage for shady gardens. | 4 to 8 | Partial shade. Well-drained, evenly moist soil. Sweet woodruff may spread too rapidly and become weedy in sites with abundant organic matter and moisture. |

| | | | Time of Bloom | Height & Spread | Uses | Hardiness Zones | Growing Conditions |
|---|---|---|---|---|---|---|---|
| | **TANSY**<br>*Tanacetum vulgare* | A fragrant perennial whose tall stems bear many deep green, ferny leaves with a pungent, resinous odor. The clusters of $1/3$- to $1/2$-in. flowers resemble daisies without white outer petals. Tansy oil is toxic; do not ingest. | Late summer to mid-autumn | Height: 2–4'<br><br>Spread: 1–2' | Leaves and flowers used in skin cleansing lotions and to produce yellow-green dye. Ornamental foliage and flowers repel insects. | 4 to 11 | Full sun to partial shade. Average, moist, well-drained soil. Harvest leaves starting in midsummer. |
| | **TARRAGON**<br>◂ *Artemisia dracunculus*<br>*A. dracunculus* 'Sativa' | A perennial wormwood whose narrow, 1- to 5-in., gray-green leaves have a piquant fragrance. The creamy yellow flowers, clustered in $1/8$-in. heads, are usually sterile. A. dracunculus 'Sativa' is considered to have the finest flavor. | Summer | Height: 1–3'<br><br>Spread: 1–1$1/2$' | Leaves used to flavor soups, stews, vinegar, fish, sauces, shellfish, eggs, and poultry (add near end of cooking); also used as a digestive aid. | 4 to 11 | Full sun to partial shade. Humus-rich, well-drained, sandy soil. Propagate from divisions or cuttings rather than seeds. Harvest leaves in midsummer and use fresh, frozen, or pickled in vinegar. Root rot and mildew may be problems. |
| | **THYME**<br>LEMON THYME<br>*Thymus × citriodorus*<br>COMMON THYME<br>◂ *T. vulgaris* | Shrubby perennials whose aromatic foliage is used as a culinary herb. T. vulgaris has gray-green, oval, evergreen leaves and loose clusters of small lilac flowers. T. × citriodorus has glossy dark green or variegated leaves with a lemon scent. | Late spring to summer | Height: 6–12"<br><br>Spread: 6–12" | Leaves used to season salads, sauces, spreads, fish, and poultry, and in herbal baths and skin lotions. | 6 to 9 | Full sun to partial shade. Well-drained soil of average fertility. Grow thyme species as annuals north of zone 6. Sow seeds $1/4$ in. deep in mid-spring. Harvest leaves as needed. |
| | **THYME**<br>CREEPING THYME<br>*Thymus praecox*<br>WILD THYME<br>◂ *T. serpyllum* | Shrubby perennials often grown as aromatic ground covers. Use the fragrant, $1/4$-in. leaves as a substitute for common thyme. Lilac or rosy, tubular, $1/4$-in. flowers grow in $1/2$-in. clusters at tips of hairy stems. | Late spring to early summer | Height: 1–4"<br><br>Spread: 1–2' | Leaves used like those of common thyme. Ornamental ground cover for walks and rock gardens. | 5 to 9 | Full sun to partial shade. Well-drained soil of average fertility. Creeping thyme grows well in spaces between stones in walks and rock gardens. Plants spread slowly. |
| | **VALERIAN**<br>GARDEN HELIOTROPE<br>*Valeriana officinalis* | Herbaceous perennial grown for its aromatic roots and flowers. Clusters of strongly perfumed, creamy white or pinkish, $1/4$- to $1/3$-in., funnel-shaped flowers top tall, leafy stems. Leaves are deeply divided, attached in pairs to the stem. | Late spring to mid-summer | Height: 3–5'<br><br>Spread: 6–18" | Roots used in calming herbal teas and herbal bath. | 4 to 8 | Full sun to light shade. Valerian is easy to grow and not terribly fussy about soil conditions. Plants spread rapidly by extending roots and self-seeding. Thin periodically to keep plants in control. |

◂ *Indicates species shown*

# *Herbs for American Gardens*

| | | Time of Bloom | Height & Spread | Uses | Hardiness Zones | Growing Conditions |
|---|---|---|---|---|---|---|
| **VETIVER** KHUS-KHUS *Vetiveria zizanioides* | A perennial grass whose aromatic roots can be used to make baskets. The stiff, 3- to 5-ft. leaves bend at an angle about a foot from the tips, forming a dramatic, angular clump. The fluffy flower plumes rise several feet above the leaves. | Late summer to early autumn | Height: 4–8' Spread: 2–4' | Aromatic roots used in potpourris and woven into baskets. Oil distilled from the roots used in perfumes. | 9 to 11 | Full sun to light shade. Moist, humus-rich, well-drained soil. Vetiver can be grown as an annual north of zone 9. Once established, this warm-season grass is drought tolerant and adapts to many types of soil. |
| **VIOLET** SWEET VIOLET *Viola odorata* | An old-fashioned garden favorite for its fragrant, ½-in., purple, blue, or white flowers rising on stalks above the 2-in., downy, heart-shaped leaves. The lowest of the 5 flower petals has a spur laden with nectar and sweet perfume. | Spring | Height: 4–6" Spread: 6–12" | Fresh or candied flowers used to garnish salads, soups, and beverages. Fresh and dried flowers used in potpourris and perfumes. Ornamental flowers. | 5 to 9 | Full to partial shade. Moist, humus-rich soil. Sweet violet slowly creeps by rhizome growth or self-seeding and under ideal conditions may become a bit rampant. Mildew and slugs may be problems. |
| **WITCH HAZEL** CHINESE WITCH HAZEL *Hamamelis mollis* COMMON WITCH HAZEL ◄ *H. virginiana* | Vigorous shrubs whose many cultivars provide a range of flower and leaf colors throughout the seasons. The autumn-flowering H. virginiana grows taller than the spring-flowering H. mollis. | H. mollis: Late winter to early spring H. virgin.: Autumn | H. mollis Height: 10–15' Spread: 6–12' H. virgin. Height: 15–25' Spread: 10–20' | Extract from distilled twigs used in cosmetics and astringent skin lotions. | H. mollis: 5 to 9 H. virgin.: 3 to 8 | Full sun to partial shade. Moist, well-drained, slightly acid soil rich in organic matter. No serious diseases or insect pests bother witch hazel. |
| **WORMWOOD** *Artemisia absinthium* | A perennial shrub whose silky, feathery, gray-green, 2- to 4-in. leaves were used to flavor absinthe, a liqueur now banned because it damages the nervous system. Light green flowers are clustered in ⅛-in. heads. | Mid- to late summer | Height: 2–4' Spread: 1–2' | Leaves used as insect repellent and antiseptic. Ornamental foliage. | 4 to 11 | Full sun to partial shade. Well-drained soil of low to average fertility; clay loam is best. Plant wormwood by itself; it may inhibit the growth of other plants. Prune to maintain form and encourage vigorous growth. |
| **YARROW** *Achillea millefolium* | An excellent perennial for flower beds and rock gardens. Fernlike, gray-green, 1- to 2-in. leaves are fragrant when touched. The leafy stems with flat-topped clusters of white flowers make long-lasting additions to fresh arrangements. | Late spring to late summer | Height: 1½–3½' Spread: 8–12" | Leaves and flowers used in astringent and cleansing lotions. Flowers produce a yellow dye. Ornamental foliage and flowers. | 3 to 10 | Full sun to partial shade. Moderately rich, well-drained soil. Plants tolerate hot, dry conditions; too much watering may lead to mildew problems. Most yarrows spread rapidly and should be divided periodically. |

# Plant Hardiness Zone Map

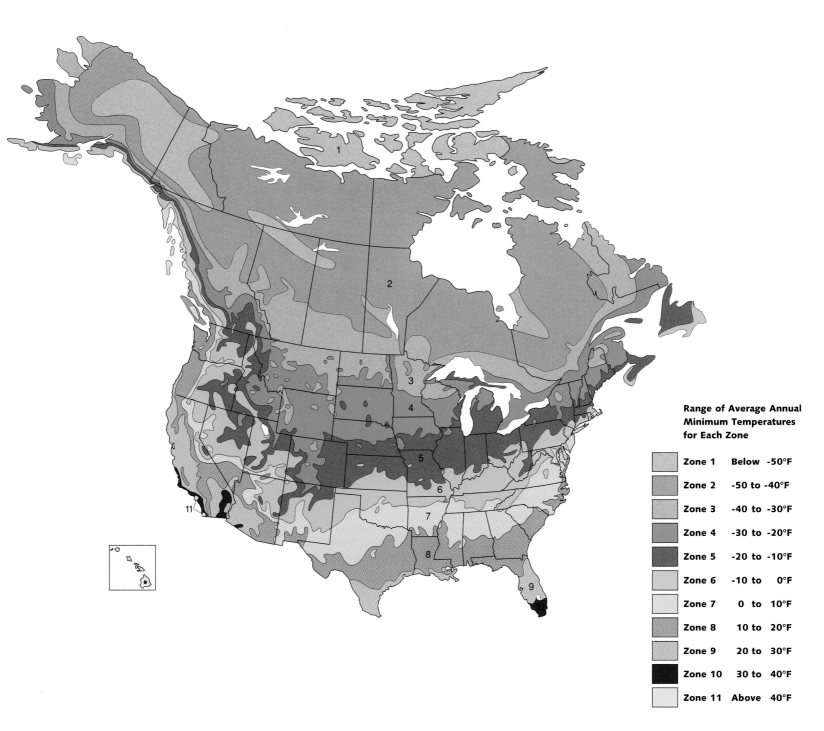

Range of Average Annual
Minimum Temperatures
for Each Zone

| | | |
|---|---|---|
| Zone 1 | Below | -50°F |
| Zone 2 | -50 to | -40°F |
| Zone 3 | -40 to | -30°F |
| Zone 4 | -30 to | -20°F |
| Zone 5 | -20 to | -10°F |
| Zone 6 | -10 to | 0°F |
| Zone 7 | 0 to | 10°F |
| Zone 8 | 10 to | 20°F |
| Zone 9 | 20 to | 30°F |
| Zone 10 | 30 to | 40°F |
| Zone 11 | Above | 40°F |

# Resources for Herb Gardening

There are many dependable mail-order suppliers that can be helpful for growing herbs. A selection is included here. Most have catalogues available upon request (some charge a fee). An excellent source of further resources is Gardening by Mail by Barbara J. Barton. Updates on each edition are provided three times a year, available through subscription (forms provided in back of book); a new edition comes out every few years. To obtain this book check your local bookstore or contact the publisher: Houghton Mifflin Co., 222 Berkeley Street, Boston, MA 02116. Telephone: (617) 351-5000.

**Plants and Seeds**

Abundant Life Seed
Foundation
P.O. Box 772
Port Townsend,
WA 98368
206-385-7192
Nonprofit foundation that
sells over 600 varieties of
open-pollinated, chemical-
free seeds.

W. Atlee Burpee Co.
300 Park Avenue
Warminster, PA 18974
215-674-4900
Seeds and supplies from
one of the oldest names in
American gardening.

Capriland's Herb Farm
534 Silver Street
Coventry, CT 06238
203-742-7244
Seeds and supplies.

Comstock, Ferre & Co.
P.O. Box 125
263 Main Street
Wethersfield, CT 06109
800-753-3773
Interesting collection of
heritage herb seeds.

The Cook's Garden
P.O. Box 535
Londonderry, VT 05148
802-824-3400
Herbs, vegetables, and
flowers. Catalogue offers a
sprinkling of recipes.

DeGiorgi Seeds & Goods
6011 'N' Street
Omaha, NE 68117-1634
800-858-2580
Herbs, vegetables, annu-
als, and perennials.

Henry Field's Seed &
Nursery Co.
415 N. Burnett Street
Shenandoah, IA 51602
605-665-9391
Seeds, supplies, and
plants.

Fox Hill Farm
P.O. Box 9
443 W. Michigan Avenue
Parma, MI 49269
517-531-3179
Over 400 herbs, including
rare varieties.

Gurney's Seed &
Nursery Co.
110 Capital Street
Yankton, SD 57079
605-665-1930
Seeds, plants, and fertilizers for herb, flower, and
vegetable gardeners.

Harris Seeds
60 Saginaw Drive
P.O. Box 22960
Rochester, NY 14692
716-442-0100
Many varieties of herb,
vegetable, and flower
seeds as well as seed-
starting equipment.

Hillary's Garden
P.O. Box 430
Warwick, NY 10990-0430
914-987-1175
Organically grown herbs
direct from the grower.

Johnny's Selected Seeds
Foss Hill Road
Albion, ME 04910-9731
207-437-4301
Vegetables, herbs, flowers,
supplies, and books for
gardeners.

Mellinger's Inc.
2310 W. South Range Rd.
North Lima, OH 44452
800-321-7444
Seeds, plants, supplies,
and tools.

Nichols Garden Nursery
1190 N. Pacific Highway
Albany, OR 97321-4598
503-928-9280
Herbs and rare seeds,
as well as books and
supplies.

Park Seed Co.
Cokesbury Road
Greenwood, SC 29647
803-845-3369
Seeds, plants, bulbs, tools,
and a wide selection of
gardening supplies.

Richters
357 Highway 47
Goodwood, Ontario
Canada LOC 1AO
416-640-6677
Seeds for many herbs and
vegetables.

Seeds of Change
P.O. Box 15700
Sante Fe, NM
87506-5700
505-438-8080
Organic seeds, including
herbs, vegetables, and
flowers.

Shepherd's Garden Seeds
6116 Highway 9
Felton, CA 95018
For advice: 408-335-6910
To order: 203-482-3638
Herbs and vegetables,
including gourmet vari-
eties. Selected recipes.

Stokes Seeds, Inc.
Box 548
Buffalo, NY 14240-0548
716-695-6980
Vegetable seeds and sup-
plies for commercial farm-
ers and home gardeners.

Thompson & Morgan
P.O. Box 1308
Jackson, NJ 08527-0308
800-274-7333
Seeds of all types and a
wide range of garden
supplies.

Tom Thumb Workshops
RR 1
Mappsville, VA 23407
804-824-3507
Herbs, spices, wreaths,
and potpourris.

The Thyme Garden
20546 Alsea Highway
Alsea, OR 97324
503-487-8671
Herb seeds. Catalogue
includes history, uses,
folklore, and recipe
section.

Well-Sweep Herb Farm
317 Mt. Bethel Road
Port Murray, NJ 07865
908-852-5390
Seeds, supplies, gifts, and
books.

## Regional Specialties

High Altitude Gardens
P.O. Box 1048
Hailey, ID 83333
208-788-4363
Seeds selected for their
ability to grow at high
altitudes.

Ed Hume Seeds, Inc.
P.O. Box 1450
Kent, WA 98035
206-859-1110
Untreated flower, herb,
and vegetable seeds for
short-season climates.

Kilgore Seed Co.
1400 W. First Street
Sanford, FL 32771
407-323-6630
Seeds selected for their
ability to grow in Florida,
Gulf Coast states, and
other tropical and sub-
tropical areas.

Native Seeds/SEARCH
2509 N. Campbell #325
Tucson, AZ 85719
602-327-9123
Native seeds of the
Southwest and Mexico,
propagated with preserva-
tion in mind; distributed
free to Native Americans.

Redwood City Seed Co.
P.O. Box 361
Redwood City, CA 94064
415-325-7333
Heirloom vegetables and
herbs, including Asian and
Native American varieties.

Southern Exposure Seed
Exchange
P.O. Box 158
North Garden, VA 22959
804-973-4703
Seeds for southern
gardens.

## Supplies & Accessories

Alsto's Handy Helpers
P.O. Box 1267
Galesburg, IL 61401
800-447-0048
A selection of tools and
other gardening
equipment.

Earth-Rite
Zook & Ranck, Inc.
RD 1, Box 243
Gap, PA 17527
800-332-4171
Fertilizers and soil
amendments for lawn
and garden.

Garden Way, Inc.
102nd St. & 9th Ave.
Troy, NY 12180
800-833-6990
Mowers, rotary tillers,
garden carts, and other
lawn and garden
equipment.

Gardener's Eden
P.O. Box 7303
San Francisco, CA 94120
800-822-9600
Many items appropriate
for gardeners, including
outdoor containers, tools,
and accessories.

Gardener's Supply Co.
128 Intervale Road
Burlington, VT 05401
800-688-5510
Tools, supplies, and equipment for gardening.

Gardens Alive!
5100 Schenley Place
Lawrenceburg, IN 47025
812-537-8650
Beneficial insects and a
complete line of supplies
for organic gardening.

Home Gardener
Manufacturing Company
30 Wright Avenue
Lititz, PA 17543
800-880-2345
Composting and related
gardening equipment.

Kemp Company
160 Koser Road
Lititz, PA 17543
800-441-5367
Shredders, chippers, and
other power equipment.

MacKenzie Nursery
Supply, Inc.
P.O. Box 322
Perry, OH 44081
800-777-5030
Large collection of tools
and supplies.

Walt Nicke's Garden Talk
P.O. Box 433
36 McLeod Lane
Topsfield, MA 01983
800-822-4114
Catalogue featuring over
300 tools and products.

The Perfect Season
P.O. Box 191
McMinnville, TN 37110
615-668-3225
Herbs and various garden
accessories.

Plow & Hearth
P.O. Box 830
Orange, VA 22960
800-866-6072
Gardening tools and prod-
ucts as well as garden
ornaments and furniture.

Ringer Corporation
9959 Valley View Road
Eden Prairie, MN 55344
612-941-4180
Organic soil amendments,
beneficial insects, and garden tools.

Smith & Hawken
Two Arbor Lane
Box 6900
Florence, KY 41022-6900
800-776-3336
Well-crafted tools as well
as containers, supplies,
and furniture.

# Index

**Photo Credits**

All photography credited as follows is copyright © 1994 by the individual photographers. **Rita Buchanan:** pp. 38 (top right), 39 (center), 74 (right), 80; **Karen Bussolini:** pp. 12, 14, 24, 39 (top left), 68, 79, 104; **David Cavagnaro:** pp. 7, 38 (left), 39 (right); **Walter Chandoha:** pp. 13, 52, 61, 101 (bottom); **Rosalind Creasy:** pp. 28, 35 (left), 37 (right), 38 (bottom right), 74 (left, center), 75 (all); **Christine M. Douglas:** pp. 4, 10, 27 (top), 41 (red beebalm), 62, 92, 96; **Derek Fell:** pp. 23 (top right), 32, 67, 105; **Dency Kane:** pp. 9, 36 (left), 40 (all), 41 (goldenrod), 84, 88; **Maggie Oster:** pp. 15, 22, 42-43; **Jerry Pavia:** pp. 37 (left), 58; **Susan Roth:** pp. 18, 27 (bottom), 31 (bottom right), 72; **Steven Still:** pp. 30, 36 (center), 41 (creeping thyme); 57; **Joseph G. Strauch, Jr.:** pp. 36 (right), 39 (bottom left); **Michael S. Thompson:** pp. 41 (beebalm 'Croftway Pink', borage, valerian), 106; **Cynthia Woodyard:** pp. 19, 20, 29 (all), 34, 35 (right), 54, 56, 82.

Step-by-step photography by Derek Fell.

Front cover photograph copyright © 1994 by Maggie Oster.

All plant encyclopedia photography is copyright © 1994 by **Derek Fell**, except the following, which are copyright © 1994 by the individual photographers. **Saxon Holt:** elecampane *(Inula helenium);* **Dency Kane:** betony *(Stachys officinalis),* catnip *(Nepeta cataria),* horehound *(Marrubium vulgare),* mint marigold *(Tagetes lucida),* pennyroyal *(Mentha pulegium);* **Elvin McDonald:** Corsican mint *(Mentha requienii);* **Jerry Pavia:** fennel *(Foeniculum vulgare);* **Steven Still:** angelica *(Angelica archangelica);* **Joseph G. Strauch, Jr.:** mugwort *(Artemisia vulgaris),* perilla *(Perilla frutescens),* rue *(Ruta graveolens),* witch hazel *(Hamamelis virginiana).*